My friend, Kitten.

Bella, Holly & Amy

Copyright © Bella, Holly & Amy 2024

The Author has asserted their rights under the Copyright Act 1968 (the Act) to be identified as the author of this work.

All rights reserved. No part of this publication may be reproduced, stored in a retrieval system, or transmitted in any form or by any means, electronic, mechanical, photocopying, recording or otherwise, without the prior written permission of the author. Any person who does any unauthorised act in relation to this publication may be liable to criminal prosecution and civil claims for damages.

The Australian Copyright Act 1968 (the Act) allows a maximum of one chapter or ten per cent of this book, whichever is the greater, to be photocopied for educational purposes by an educational institution holding a statutory education licence provided that the educational institution (or body that administers it) has given a remuneration notice to the Copyright Agency (Australia) under the Act.

ISBN: 978-1923163-36-2 (Paperback)

A catalogue record for this book is available from the National Library of Australia

Format and Typesetting: Clark & Mackay
Cover Design: Bella, Holly & Amy and Clark & Mackay

Self-Published by Bella, Holly & Amy with assistance from Clark & Mackay
Proudly printed in Australia by Clark & Mackay

Play Zed, 'Renegade Fighter'

Buckle up baby, you're in for a wild ride …

Ima rock your world.

—*Kitten*

Sadly, this is a true story; however: names, dates, places, and any other definitive information has been changed or omitted. Nevertheless, if anyone recognises the true SECRET identity of any of the people, please keep it confidential!!

There are things in here that will shake you to your very core.

Introductions

Bella/ (Kitten)

Heya, I'm Isabelle. My nickname is Kitten, I am the mastermind and lead author. I've had some really terrible bad stuff happen to me, and I give you fair warning, there is some pretty heavy stuff in here. I did my best to make my book as readable as possible. Ultimately; this is an inspiring adventurous, uplifting story of triumph.

This story is about me and my life. I was born unlikeable, unloveable and hideous, apparently barely tolerable. Not even my own mother ever liked, loved or wanted me. When I was a little a girl I was always alone.

If I wasn't alone, I was being yelled at by my mummy (my only family) who made sure I knew I wasn't loved, liked or wanted. She belittled and made fun of me in front of and with her friends, or I was being beaten, tortured, raped and worse by the nine disgusting men in a paedophile ring across the road. Honestly the latter was the better option because at least I got some attention and acknowledgment. My own mum not liking me was far more painful.

I never really was a child or had a childhood. Apart from my inherent maturity and intellect, I was molested for the first time at age 3 by a man I called 'uncle' who lived in my nanna's complex while his wife, my 'auntie', sat there watching and did nothing to stop it. Being alone and subjected to adult things from a young age made me grow up fast. I was bathing and dressing myself by 5 years old.

You can't imagine how badly I hurt sometimes. There are times/minutes/moments of pain so sharp, intense and unbearable, if there was a gun next to me, I'd pick it up and end it all without hesitation. They say God doesn't allow suicides into heaven, but I'm pretty sure he'd make an exception for me after everything I've endured!

I have scars on my wrists from suicide attempts, scars on my heart from all the people who hurt me and scars on my body from the horrible things that have happened to me and all the times I cut and burnt myself. People stare at my scars sometimes and look at me with pity and disgust. It's embarrassing, but I know they don't understand.

A small child rejected by her own mother for a start, shattered my poor sweet little heart. I remember standing on the street curb between the two houses, looking back at my home and knowing if I went there my mummy would either ignore me or yell at me, often for things I hadn't even done.

The other choice was to go to my friend's house and possibly (it didn't happen every time; sometimes we just got to play and be kids) be exploited, used and hurt. I often chose the second choice because at least in a strange way, I felt wanted and accepted. I got attention and even though it was mostly bad at least I felt part of something and wasn't alone. Any child starved for love and affection, will choose any attention over none.

When I was very small, before those men beat the ability to cry out of me, I used to wander off alone and find a place to sit in a tiny ball of broken-hearted neglected child and cry my little eyes out wondering why I was so horrible, and no one liked or wanted me. I would cry so hard I could barely breathe, sobbing so hard my entire body was shaking.

As an adult, I have serious issues with trust, relationships, and all forms of affection, touch and intimacy, even just friendship. I can barely stand to be touched, I struggle with feelings of worthlessness and sometimes have to fight severe depression. Suicidal thoughts still cross my mind, and occasionally on my bad days I'll pick up a knife to cut some fruit and have to fight the urge to drive it into myself or drag the blade across my skin, but these are behaviours I'm fighting and trying to conquer.

I am a unique, talented private counsellor and human being and I care for everyone fiercely. I've always felt like I never really belonged, always separate, which is possibly my own doing and a distance I created in my own mind.

I am going to change the world and save lives, change lives, educate and make a difference and my drive comes from the deepest, sharpest suffering. I know what and how it feels to be scared, to hurt and to be alone and I understand the repercussions of abuse through years of dissecting every nuance and side effect of what I went through. I don't want anyone else to ever feel even a tiny fraction of the sadness and pain I felt and still feel.

I am gentle and quite literally wouldn't hurt a fly: I vacuum up cockroaches and set them free outside instead of killing them. I stand up for people and what's right, even if it gets me hurt instead and I would die protecting someone or fighting for right and justice if the need arose. I help people see their awesome and lift them up.

Sometimes I try too hard, but I don't care, I see everything so clearly and I want to help everyone. I am the one person I can't help, the one little girl whose pain I can't stop or lessen, the one heart I can't unbreak and the one person I can't put back together. Some people are mean and take advantage of or treat me badly, but I steadfastly refuse to let anyone else's bad behaviour change my pure Angel heart.

Helping and healing others distracts me and makes me feel worthy. I have painstakingly collected all the little pieces of my shattered being over the years. I have them in a little basket I take everywhere and keep very safe in case I meet someone whose love can heal me. I was too efficient in creating a life that distances me from others, one where I can be alone so no one can hurt me anymore.

I am still trying to learn to like myself, to accept myself and forgive myself. Coming from a loveless, barren childhood of neglect, devoid of affection, attention and love, being made to feel hated and unwanted, barely tolerated, is a hard thing to change.

My two best friends who you will meet next, Holly and Amy, have stood by my side over the years through the stormy hellish darkness and rain, through my internal war and helped me to see I'm actually pretty Kool. Just for the record, I'm as fun as they say I am - trouble follows me everywhere nipping at my heels, giggling and urging my crazy to wake up and come out to play. My superpowers are love and confidence and somehow not dying when I climb and then fall off high things drunk, which happens far too often.

People have always come to me for advice ever since I was a teenager, it comes naturally to me. I still have the most horrible nightmares. When I was little, I imagined if I hurt myself first it might hurt less when others hurt me. Now I've turned it around. I try to love myself because I genuinely can't stand to have others care about or love me. It's a truly petrifying alien landscape which I greatly fear.

There will be someone who can heal me one day when the time is right. They will fight hard until I give in. Until that day, I will work on changing the world one person at a time by spreading love, light, kindness and leading by example.

I am so different now then I was, always being used, pushed aside, neglected, and treated badly most of my life, like I didn't matter. I struggled to stand up for myself, but I could always fight for and stand up for others easily and my confidence grew in helping and protecting them. It's been really hard for me with my inappropriate, flirty, affectionate personality, but now I have fire in me. My nickname might be Kitten, but I've discovered I'm actually a tiger.

By the end of this, I hope you will be immensely proud of the kind, loving, strong, overprotective, confident Kitten I am today. I am and that's a huge thing coming from me. Despite the truly atrocious, disturbing and disgusting parts of my chapter in this novel, I hope my writing style softens it and you are ultimately captivated, intensely inspired, and really enjoy reading this.

>Oodles of love,
>Always and forever,
>Yours and yours alone,
>Bella

Amy/Bunny

Yeah, so this is the one and fucking *only* lil miss bunny wabbit, Amy. Holly and Bella are tight, but Kit's like my family, we are each other's family. We have a special love, like unique, not just gay for fuck's sake! But, well, teehee that too.

I'm a tiny 5 ft.2 and not very smart but I can be fun and I always stick up for my friends. My parents can't stand me, so no one ever wanted me, except Kitten, she saved me!

I used to have bad problems with drugs, alcohol and eating disorders. Kit helped me and now I'm good. We always have parties at my parents' place; they are never home.

I'm not very important, but Kit gets me and knows me. She connects with lots of people and makes everyone feel special, but I know I'm actually special to her, like for real. I'm so fucking lucky, I can't believe how lucky I am: I get to know her and be close to her. I swear a lot, get used to it. You get to read my chapter first, lucky fucking you.

Life with Kitten is so weird, fun, crazy and exciting.

Loads of fucking kisses,
Bunny

Holly

So, Isabella asked us to write our own introductions. Our chapters, although written in our words, have been edited by her to match the style she writes in, however these are our words only. Not sure that's the best idea, but still … I am a few years older than Kitten, we used to model together way back in Nam.

We met in Surfers and were together for years before we realised we knew each other from modelling. Yep, so blonde I know. I am smart and hot and wild too, so we are a perfect match.

We are both elegant, sophisticated, and classy. We know it, own it, flaunt it. When we walk down the street together, heads turn, boys crash cars and wives get angry at perving husbands. They needn't worry, we are soulmates completely engrossed in one another. I've never wanted anyone else's attention and why would I when I have the sexiest woman alive?

Amy and I are helping her write this book so it's a bit easier for y'all to read. But you really can't understand unless you have met her and spent time with her. She's truly magic and extraordinarily amazing, generous and kind. She tries to help, heal, inspire and uplift everyone she meets. She is so incredibly loving, forgiving and understanding. I really don't know how she doesn't just spontaneously combust with all that fire and magic within. I've never met anyone so intelligent and mature, dead set. You will soon discover for yourself that Amy and I are entirely besotted and obsessed with her, as are the lucky few people who she lets get close to her. We fought hard to save her from the pain.

You have to make every second with Kitten count, you never know if it's the last time you'll ever see her again. Every time your phone rings suddenly in the middle of the night, your heart pounds feverishly with intense abject fear and you can't breathe until you know she's ok. I am passionate about psychology and sports and love music. There's nothing else you need to know about me. This is her story, her victory, over and out.

Holly A.

Jay

Bruv, dis is Jasper, but I hate that name coz my sister used to call me Jasper the lonely ghost. So peeps call me JayZ (Jay). My friend, Kitten asked me to write something for her book that wasn't so over the top like the girls did. She said to me, 'say something bad about me would you?'

So here goes, not that there's much bad to say. She literally walks her sexy lil butt around trying to change the world and lift people up; no matter how many times people kick dirt in her face or betray her, she just keeps going. Keeps loving and giving and shining.

She thinks she's fat and ugly; it's annoying because she gets upset about it a lot and it's frustrating! She's not but she can't see it, she can't see or accept any of the good or beauty in herself. She's one of the most beautiful girls I've ever seen, absolute stunner. Owns every room she walks into, her energy is enchanting and addictive.

Sometimes it's also annoying being out with her. She won't ever turn her back on someone that needs help and makes everyone's problems her own. It makes it hard to get stuff done sometimes. It can be embarrassing when she goes up and hugs a stranger, not everyone receives that well. Most people smile and hug her back gratefully, but occasionally it will upset someone and geeez if we walk past a fisherman, OMG seriously! She will scold and lecture them. That's embarrassing, but she has a valid point... poor innocent little fishies.

Oh aight, here's a good one! She's too smart and headstrong and can come across as bossy and sometimes loses patience with slow people. She seems condescending even though it's not her intention. That's embarrassing. Aight that was my best shot wit dat on to da important stuff!

Kit and my big sis Nat have been friends since first kindergarten. My dad was an asshole, he drank and beat us up. Kit was my first crush. She used to come over in little midriff tops and tiny miniskirts.

One day after a bad day at school… bullies had stolen my lunch for the third day in a row and I was starving. I rode into the yard jumped off my bike and ran inside to eat and hug my mum. I was stuffing my face when I heard my dad's car pull up outside. I shot mum a 'hope he's sober' look, but seconds later he screamed my name, yelling about my bike in the driveway.

Kit and Nat were painting nails in Nat's room. Dad came into the house yelling and fuming. The first thing I saw was my bike chain - my bike was wrecked! Mum saved up for years to get me that bike. I started to cry. He stormed over, grabbed me by my shirt and yelled in my face that I was useless and pathetic.

I was crying hard; I was so devoed about my bike. Behind him I saw Nat's door open a crack and Kit's little eye looking out. I was real embarrassed. Dad tightened his grip on my shirt front choking me, and raised his fist with my bike chain wrapped around his knuckles. I took a deep breath and tensed up ready for the blow to my face, terrified and shaking. I already had scars on my face from Dad's thrashings, but Kitten came running out of Nat's room with her bedside lamp and smacked my dad in the head with it repeatedly until he fell down. She saved my life.

I was 9 and she was almost 11, still a kid herself. When she was sure Dad was unconscious, she scooped me up and carried me outside. We sat there with me crying in her arms while da police came. She held me, sang to me, rocked and reassured me, and promised to get my bike fixed. My dad finally went to jail, my bike got fixed and Kit worked with me.

I hate to brag, but I'm every girl's dream guy. She taught me to be the best man I could; she taught me how to be and behave like a gentleman, to be protective of and treat women properly.

There's a secret I wanna tell you guys which no one else knew until now. There's a strip of forest near where I live. One day I was riding home and as I got close to the forest, I heard a girl scream. I skidded to a stop and listened hard, another scream. I thought it was a scream of pain, so I got my phone out, typed 000 and went in for a closer look. I told you, Kit raised me right. No decent man would walk away from a girl screaming.

I didn't know what to expect, so I put my bike against a tree in case I needed to fight. I kept walking and after a while I could hear soft whimpering, I'd come to a clearing, and there was a girl on her knees in the middle facing away. There was shit loads of blood on the grass near me. I looked around for whoever did this, aware he still could be hiding nearby. I was tense and on high alert, I called 000, explained and requested police and ambulance. I walked around slowly until I was facing her. I was totes shitting myself. I didn't know what I was going to find when I looked up.

I took a deep breath and tried to make myself man up, but I couldn't do it, not after seeing all that blood and way too many horror movies. I argued with myself in my head, but I couldn't.

I was trying to listen for movement around me in case he was still here. She was still whimpering, so she was alive at least, but probably not for much longer after losing all that blood! I heard sirens in the distance getting closer quickly.

I relax a little and forced myself to look up. To my absolute shock and dismay, I saw Kitten next to a bloody knife. Her forearms had long, deep gashes in them, blood was everywhere. I was still on edge expecting an attack any second. My muscles tensed and fists clenched ready. I looked around properly; her skateboard was resting up against a tree next to an empty bottle of rum. I looked at her closely; she was kind of slumping, maybe from loss of blood, maybe from alcohol, maybe from pain.

I heard the police and ambos turn off their sirens but could hear the sound of cars driving at speed, so I knew they were close. I ran over yelling her name and that I was here, that she was safe. She didn't hear me.

I was halfway there when she got the knife and sliced it across her skin. Blood spurted - I was so confused; I didn't realise what was happening until it was too late.

I yelled, 'No, Bella!' and got down quickly, removing the knife from her hand. I ripped my shirt off, trying to stem the blood that was spurting everywhere.

I screamed for the emergency service guys and they yelled they were coming, and for the seven-ish minutes it took them to find us, she cried in my arms. She looked into my eyes and whispered, 'Jay, sometimes I hurt so bad,' then didn't say anything else, just bawled so hard till they found us, holding me so dam tight. I hid the knife in my pocket then there was a flurry of activity. Police secured the perimeter apparently, I'm not quite sure how they managed that in a forest though lol, and then ambos came.

They took her away and I went with her to hospital, holding her paw in the back of the ambulance. They kept asking what had happened, but she was completely silent, and I just said I came across her like that in the clearing. I knew she'd tried to kill herself, but I didn't say a word.

They kept her in for a week on psych hold because she wouldn't say a single thing to anyone other than me. I practically lived there. She was a bit under 16, it was so strange. She never showed any signs of sadness, was constantly bubbly and vibrant, always the happy centre of attention wherever she went. Giggly, loud, crazy fun and then BOOM out of nowhere this happened.

We never spoke of it again after, I don't even think she remembers crying, which from what I hear, is probably a good thing. I never told anyone this until now. Only me, Kit, her mum and the ambos/ hospital staff knew; only I know she tried to die. She'd drunk an entire bottle of straight rum herself and she was still only a teenager, but she actually cried, and I'll never forget being that close to her for that time. I am the man I am today because of you, Kitten. I feel honoured she chose to trust me enough to let go just that once. When we hug, we are so close and hold each other so tight. She is the yin to my yang, but it's not reciprocated.

At school, the boys used to bully me, I'm pretty skinny and used to be dorky; they would steal my stuff and food and push me around. The day with my dad and bike, I told her about it. So she started bringing me lunch at school sometimes.

One day she came to school bringing me a pizza for lunch. She looked so cute and hot as she strutted up in her sketchers and pigtails. All the boys were looking - some whistled.

She came over and gave me my lunch then loudly asked me if I'd kissed a girl yet. I was almost 14 and hadn't. I was so embarrassed; all the other boys had and when I said no, she leant in and kissed me, pulling me forward so we were pressed up against each other. I got hard instantly, then she put my hands on her tits and I almost creamed my pants. The boys were cheering loudly, it was awesome, when she stepped back, I quickly sat down to hide my boner with a huge smile on my face.

Then she asked loudly, 'Which boys have been picking on you?' I pointed them out. She walked over turned and said, 'Jay, wanna be my boyfriend?' I was starving and had started stuffing my face with pizza, so I nodded. She turned back to the guys and said to them, 'If you bother my boyfriend ever again, I will come here and kick the living crap out of you. Got it?' They all stuttered they wouldn't and that was the end of the bullying.

I was no longer a lonely ghost, I was a legend. No one used to come to my birthday parties, but after that day everyone wanted to come; Kit helped me make them naughty and fun. I wasn't a loner or loser anymore; I was cool and popular. I wasn't really her boyfriend, she said that would have been weird and I was too young, but I wanted to be.

As I got older and spent more time with my sister's group of friends, I saw stuff and heard stuff. Then once I read this, I understood it all, it made me really angry and I wanted to go after them and hurt them, but when I was younger, Kitten taught me women don't like anger or violence, it scares them. They want to feel safe, understood and protected. So instead, I took her in my arms and held her tight and close and told her, 'I'm so sorry you were hurt. I'm here, you're safe and I'll protect you always.'

I've known Bella longer than Holly or Amy, and I watched her make everyone who wanted to get close to her prove themselves over and over again. I never had to do that, maybe because I grew up with her, or maybe I proved it with my actions over all these years. I've always had her back, always helped and been there for her.

Being with Kitten is like being with yourself, but way more fun. You can be 100% yourself always, and you know you'll always be seen, heard, accepted, loved and adored. She has this old skool polite, proper way of speaking and behaving and always does the right thing, with class. For example, she hand-writes and gives thank you cards, says things like: 'may I? My sincerest apologies, thank you for having me, please forgive and excuse my behaviour/mistake,' and other weird, proper, elegant English phrases, but she makes it look and sound cute and Kool.

You will never hear her swear or use the Lord's name for anything other than praise and prayer. She helps old people cross the street, carries older people's grocery bags for them, that sort of thing. Then on the complete reverse of that, when she's just with us, she's wild and crazy and hella fun. She once did topless bikini mudwrestling at a concert. She was 14, and she got on the TV and in the newspaper for her craziness that year.

Chapter One
Amy (Bunny)

Hola, I'm Amy but Kit calls me Bunny (coz I'm tiny, cute, (and just a little bit fluffy). My friend, Kitten is the best person I know. Have you heard of body dysmorphia? Kind of like: looking in the mirror and seeing something gross and awful when you look at yourself. Well, she doesn't just have body dysmorphia she has entire person dysmorphia. She thinks she is fat, ugly, horrible, worthless and unlovable.

She can turn even the dullest boring things into a fun, interesting adventure with her craziness and wild caring heart. Even a casual trip to the shops is thrilling and we often leave with a few new friends. People are drawn to her cheekiness, brightness, smile and confidence.

She is easy to take advantage of because she is too kind and generous. I see it all the time; it drives me fucking loco. Someone will need money or her time or help, whatever and Kitten will literally drop everything and be there for someone in need, but then they don't pay her back or they take advantage of her kindness, the knob heads.

She just gives them another chance, helps them again and again. We had another girl in our group called Shelly who used to do this all the time the nasty bitch. One day, Kitten asked Shelly for something, and she flat out said, 'No.' Kit is strong, but if you watch her real close, you can see the sadness in her eyes.

I was right next to her and saw the tiny flinch of her eyes and knew that hurt her feelings, so I said, 'go on, Shel, you kind of owe her.' She ignored me, so I took a fairly big run up, crash tackled the stupid slut into the pool we were standing around, fully clothed, $3000 designer handbag, cell phone and all! She umm doesn't hang out with us anymore, but Kitten looked at me and held my gaze for a moment and something real passed between us. Then she smiled and I knew I was right. Kit is our protector mainly, but she needs protecting too sometimes. Even though she hides it, it still hurts her when someone lets her down, which happens a lot. I felt so proud of myself that day. It's so hard to get close to her.

There are a different set of rules for Bella. She gets away with things the rest of us wouldn't, like being cheeky and insolent to police officers. Talking to and hugging complete strangers, whistling and calling out, 'Oi, sexy,' when attractive people walk past, climbing random things drunk in the middle of the night and always ending up in the hospital or police station a couple times a week. Her sense of adventure gets her in trouble a lot. But everyone loves her. She is always unapologetically, inappropriately and very loudly herself. She smiles and laughs and hides her sadness and how hard she has to fight every day, but I see it.

You have to watch Kitten carefully her poker face is way too good. If she's really struggling, she won't tell you, she will hide away in the pain and silently, slowly slip away from you. If you aren't watching closely, if you miss the signs, then one day you will realise you're looking at a ghost, that Kitten actually left with the tide a long time ago, leaving you with an empty robot on automatic. You have to be so gentle with Kitten, you can't get angry or upset with her to her face, she can't handle it. You have to understand she needs reassurance that you like her and care and that she's not completely horrible and hideous.

Sometimes she needs you to be there next to her quietly while she fights an inner war. You have to appreciate how hard she tries every single day not to let her sadness show. She thinks this makes her harder to love. That she's unlovable. She is so easy to love but cannot see that.

One night, Holly rings me at 11:30. There is a smile in her voice as she says, 'Bunny, get up, get dressed - we need to conduct an emergency rescue mission.'

I laugh and sigh. 'What's she done now?' Holly doesn't tell me.

It turns out Kitten had got herself tangled while climbing a rollercoaster (as you do) and was stuck somehow. We pull up at the theme park and crack up laughing at the sight of Kitten dangling from the side of the roller coaster. I take a few pictures on my phone, then we get to work, Charlie's Angels style. Holly climbs up and yells back that we have to turn the ride on. OMG, I'm scared as but I don't let it show.

Kit yells out directions and thankfully it's easy. I turn the ride on and slowly bring the train carriage thingys down till her feet touch the ground, then Holly climbs up and unhooks her bracelet. Once she's free, I turn to her and say, 'Umm, Kitten - What? How? WHY????'

She hugs me. 'Spank you my lil Bunny.' Stretching her aching arms, she says, 'I was stuck up there, clinging on to the side for like an hour. 'I reply 'Again, why? How did you even get here?'

There's no answer. She just sighs deeply and looks up at the stars with glistening eyes. We walk to the car, and I put my arms around her. 'Are you ok, baby gurl?' Her silence confirms what I already know, she's not ok.

She is my superhero; just being around her is intoxicating. She is effortlessly sexy, always in sexy elegant dresses and naturally beautiful, with no makeup required. She's the epitome of a perfect human being. She talks to and hugs total strangers in the street if she thinks they look sad. If she sees a child alone, she stays with them until they are safe. She makes sure everyone she knows feels good about themselves and knows their worth.

She's honest and open about how she feels about us and how much we matter. I know that when she was little something bad happened. Kit knows what it's like to hurt, to be abandoned and she doesn't want anyone else to feel like that. She says her 'hearts big enough to love the whole world and her shoulders are strong enough to carry all those who need it'.

Her love has no boundaries, no limitations, and no discriminations. Her love encompasses all, no matter how they've treated her or if they deserve it or not. She sees the best in everyone and helps them see it too. She makes me smile and she makes me feel strong when I think of her. There is nothing she won't do for someone, anyone in need.

Hanging out with her is always fun; everyone knows her, says hi and has a smile and wave. But it can be annoying.

One night we are having dinner at central and a bunch of girls run across the road giggling and screaming her name. Then they are all over us, asking what's on and where are we going. (Kitten knows all the club owners and bouncers; we never have to pay or line up, always get VIP treatment and free drinks.)

She smiles and says, 'Hey girls. I'm having dinner with my friend; then we are going to a friend's private birthday sorry.' One of them asks my name and it distracts me for a sec. When I look back, Kit's making out with a redhead. 'Oi,' I say and kick her under the table. I'm jealous; I want her to like me. I want to be close to her and after a few drinks, I tell her that. She smiles at me and says, 'don't worry, princess. You are special to me.' That's her private nickname for me.

My parents are shitty parents. They don't care about me or my little brother Jack; we were always left to fend for ourselves. They took Jack away when he was just shy of 4 after the third time he almost died because of our parents' negligence. From the moment I met Kitten, I knew we were kindred souls, we always had a special secret family-like bond. From the moment I met her, I wanted to be exactly like her.

She radiates sex appeal. She is cheeky, flirty and naughty always. Everyone who meets her adores her. All the boys and most girls want her. I desperately want her attention. I try to be cheeky and flirty too; I can't pull it off like her and Kit gets angry at me. She tells me I have to be careful. I try harder coz I want to impress her; I want to be like her.

She keeps telling me to stop, that I can't be like that with just anyone and says that I come across as easy.

I stop doing it around her and the girls, but I still do it with my other friends. One day this guy starts paying attention to me and I think I'm getting better, so I flirt like she does and say sexy things. He seems to like me; I must be getting better, he tries to kiss me, and I tell him I'm in love with someone else, a girl. He gets upset and calls me a cock tease. I have no idea what that means.

One day I walk into Holly's and it's creepily quiet, Kitten is supposed to be here too, which means there should be laughter and yelling and at least one girl screaming her name in pleasure. It's too quiet. I go into the kitchen; it's a mess like they have been cooking. The thought of Kit cooking makes me want to snort with laughter. She always says, 'I have bedroom skillz, not kitchen skills.' She's not lying; she certainly does not have kitchen skills.

I walk around to the living room. Kitten is sitting in a tight ball on the floor, and Hol is with her. I'm not sure whether to give them privacy or try to help.

Holly looks utterly terrified; she kind of flicks her head a fraction without taking her eyes off Kit. I quickly walk over and slide to the floor, Kitten goes away in her mind sometimes, gets sucked back into the hellish nightmares of her past and we are all terrified that one day we won't be able to bring her back from that dark place. That one day, her mind will shatter and let go and she will be lost to insanity, lost in the black abyss.

I try to help; I sing 'Sexy Back' by Justin Timberlake, which is Kitten's song, she is so bringing sexy back but on another level.

Kitten says something so incredibly scary that to this day, I still have nightmares about it. About not meaning to cry, but the knives hurt so much she gets scared and can't help it. Crouching on the floor with Holly trying to save Kitten, I finally understand.

My eyes meet Holly's, and she knows I understand. I couldn't fight the tears that well in my eyes and violently spill over. I can see the terror in Hol's eyes. I now got why she fought so hard and is so protective of Kit. She is looking at me sternly as if willing me not to cry. It makes it worse, and I let out a huge sob followed by tears, rivers of tears that I can't control.

It was so unfair. Holly looks at me like she's trying to use Vulcan mind tricks to kill me with her eyes, but I can't help it. The pieces all fall into place in my head. It makes me cry harder; I'd always suspected abuse but my gosh, knives.

Those looks of profound intense, fierce terror she gets on her face suddenly made perfect sense.

I put my hand in Kitten's paw and threaded my fingers through hers. I focused all the love I have for her into our entwined hands, and I cry harder. I feel a tiny flinch of Kitten's paw in my hand and she is back suddenly looking at me with concern, asking me softly why I'm crying. It stunned me into abrupt silence, but she is back safe from the darkness; she wipes my tears away and I brush my lips over her bare shoulder and her eyes meet mine intently.

In a new way, she is looking at me differently, so intensely; she gently licks her lips and bites her lower lip. I want to kiss her so bad. Holly gets up and leaves the room. Kitten's paw squeezes my hand and she pulls me closer, looks into my eyes, then leans in to kiss me.

My heart's thudding so hard, I'm sure she can hear it. I've wanted this for so long.

As our lips meet, I have fireworks going off inside me. She moans softly into our kiss and kisses me harder, more passionately. My mind flicks to Holly for a brief second, but I pull it away back to enjoying this moment.

I didn't get the full story till we started writing this together however; I was beginning to understand why Kit is so special, what she went through and what she's endured. It makes me cry harder, but if I ever needed proof that she cared about me, this was the exact moment I got it - when my tears bring her back from a deep, scary meltdown/trance state.

She kisses me again, several times, and we end up being girlfriends. It's my dream come true. I tell everyone we know about 7 times - I'm Kitten's new girlfriend. Soo fucking happy, excited, electrified, stoked. This was my idea, just FYI, to help by writing this with her. See, I'm not completely useless.

One day I'm walking through the park in the warm afternoon. I see the guy that called me a cock tease and some of his friends. I walk past them quickly and he smirks at me, then wolf whistles.

I am lost in my own thoughts about work and my brother as I walk on. I'm near a toilet block and drinking fountain, so I stop for a drink. I think I see someone from the corner of my eye. I feel uneasy and decide to jog home. I half stand up and wipe my mouth and someone grabs me by my hair from behind and drags me into the toilets. I'm screaming but I can't really move from the grasp they have on my hair. I can hardly even try to fight. Every move is painful.

'Well, well, well, if it isn't the skanky little cock tease.' I know I'm in trouble now! I reach for my phone, but it's taken from my hand and I hear it clatter against the floor; then he hits my face. 'Think you're too good for me, do ya?'

I'm too scared to say anything. He hits me again, and then he starts to pull my skirt and underwear down. 'Please,' I beg. 'I'm a virgin.' I try to push him off, but he overpowers me. I scream and he punches me hard in my stomach, so fucking hard I feel like he has broken all of my ribs and it's really painful. I can't scream anymore; I can't even talk. I can't fight; it's hard to breathe. He takes my virginity on the dirty floor of the toilet block. He kicks me as he leaves. 'Got what you deserved, didn't ya?' I pass out from the pain.

I have weird dreams of footsteps and darkness. I dream Kit and I are ninja turtles and she is the first thing on my mind when I wake up groggy, disorientated and confused in the hospital. I look around not remembering at first. The nurse tells me I've been raped and beaten. Thankfully no broken bones. I slowly start to remember and I look around, searching for Kitten and my friends. There are three male police officers and I have to go with them, but I don't want to. The nurse assures me I'll be safe.

They give me strong painkillers that space me out heaps. I tell the police my story, tears flowing fast. Suddenly, I realise that this was what Kitten was telling me all along; she's going to be so disappointed. 'Where's Kitten?' I murmur. One of the cops says, 'Ah! That's where I know you from; you didn't have a phone on you … but I can get Holly's number.'

I almost want to smile, but I can't. Of course the police know Kitten, teehee. He says that my friends are on their way. I start stressing out big time. What's Kit gonna say? I'm freaking out. It seems hours before Holly and Kit walk through the door. I'm so embarrassed and ashamed. I feel dirty, damaged and disgusting.

Kitten isn't angry or disappointed, all I see is love and concern. I'm scared for a second that she will be triggered, and I cry more but not for me. I know it's hard; I can see the distress on her face.

She goes completely ape shit and screams at the pervy old policemen who have been staring at me, then takes off her dress so I have something to wear when they won't even give me a fucking blanket, carrying me out of the police station in nothing but her tiny lacy underwear. She makes a joke about maybe getting takeaway instead, since she really isn't dressed to go out to a restaurant. Through my messed-up head, swollen lips, face and very badly bruised ribs, I laugh. It truly fucking hurts. She helps me straight away, makes me repeat every last nasty detail over and over, and she actually manages to convince me it wasn't my fault. Holly and Kitten take care of me.

One night at one of my parties, we are all sitting around eating pizza, drinking, laughing and talking. Kit is always the life of every party and has us in stitches or playing a fun and usually naughty game. I notice she has gone quiet, and I glance at her; her face is completely white and she's biting her lip and looking into the distance. I look at Holly, who is normally all over it, but she is deep in conversation with Zoe. Bloody fuck! I look back at Kitten and say her name. Her knuckles are clenched tight on the table.

Then, to my horror, I realise she's biting her lip so hard there's blood dripping down her chin! 'KITTEN!' I yell, but no one seems to notice above the music and chatter. She doesn't move. I get up and run around, wrapping my arms around her.

She is frozen and unresponsive. I don't know what to do; the blood is running harder and faster now, dripping onto her pretty dress. I do something bad, but I can't think of a single other thing. I'm so scared she is gonna bite her own lip off. I pinch her hard with both hands and bite her shoulder hard. Two things happen: Holly finally notices and Kitten flinches.

I look at her face; she's stopped biting her lip, but there's blood gushing everywhere, all over my parents' expensive virgin white table cloth. If they ever come home, I'm gonna be in shitloads of trouble for that, assuming they ever actually come home or even remember that I exist.

I look closer; her eyes are filled with tears that don't fall. Holly pushes me aside like usual. But this time, I don't let her. I was the one that saved Kitten tonight. Kit's back and flinching as Holly dabs at her lip, saying, 'you're gonna need stitches.'

Imagine being in so much emotional pain you accidentally bite through your own lip. Kit looks at me, and that look says so much. There was gratitude and affection in that look, and it makes my heart explode. I was important to her, to someone, finally. I made a positive difference for the first time ever. We have to call an ambulance coz we are all too drunk to drive. I have trouble explaining to the lady on the phone how the injury occurred, but I talk up the blood loss and we don't even have to wait that long.

The ambos pull up, and when they walk in and see her, Jake smiles and laughs, saying 'Again! Seriously, Kitten!? I saw you like two days ago. What the actual fuck have you done now?' then jokes about needing her own personal ambulance to follow her around.

A few days later Kitten thanks me, and I feel so much closer to her. We all know something really bad happened to her, but only Holly knows the details. Every now and then, she will snap at something small or go into a scary trance state or disappear completely, usually for hours. Once it was days; she ended up in a completely different state.

One day, we almost lost her to the darkness:

Holly, Kit, Zoe and I are sitting outside. Hol, Zo and I are bitching about our pervert asshole head co-worker. We are lost in our bitching session until Zoe screeches: "OMG, KITTEN! BELLAAAAAA? KITTEN!!!?" My head snaps to the side and Holly jumps up. We have never seen Kit so far gone; she's shivering, and her teeth are chattering in the warm, summer arvo sun. None of us noticed her slipping away, we try everything. Complete terror tears through me as I watch her eyes go cold; I bite her and pinch. Nothing, she starts to make a low, squealing sound like a piglet in pain or something.

Zoe is crying silently. It feels like the end; we can't break the trance. Our Kitten is gone, lost in the black abyss forever. I don't even notice Holly disappear until, all of a sudden; she's back with a bucket of ice and cold water. Suddenly I realise I've been holding my breath for ages and I get very dizzy - my vision starts to get black spots. I look at Holly's face, which is screwed up in worry and fear.

She looks fifty and I nod at the bucket, desperately searching in my mind for something else that might bring her back. Where are naked, hot large-breasted strippers when you need them hey!? For a second, I'm distracted by that funny thought and imagine the strippers rubbing their boobs all over Kit's face. That would bring her back for sure! Teehee, maybe we should keep some strippers on hand?

Hol tips the icy slush over Kitten's head and face. She instantly shrieks and then starts coughing and spluttering. I can't seem to decide between feeling happy we broke the trance or concerned she is choking. All of a sudden she's angry, as if this time she didn't even realise she'd been sucked into the 'black abyss' as she calls it. It took us about an hour we guess to get her back, but it felt like ten hours. I look at her - she is disorientated, angry and cold. We'd won, except that we hadn't; she is different in a way none of us can accurately pinpoint. Its two whole days before she says a single word, I kept seeing her looking at us angrily, her eyes full of distrust. She lost some of her light that day. That was when we realised the danger was closer than we thought ... we could actually lose her ... forever.

One day, she meets a man, but not like that, seriously … if we say, 'Ooh, look at that guy. He's soo hot,' Kit will be like, 'Eeeeww, gross. Umm, no spank you. It's a boy.' She literally says 'spank you' instead of 'thank you' everywhere, even to complete strangers. It's funny to see the look on their faces.

Anyway, she meets a man, the only man who is able to accept her as she is, love her for it and allow her to be herself without taking advantage. They click instantly as their eyes meet, but not in a romantic or sexual way. She ends up calling him Dad. She changed so much after they met, her smile was brighter, a little more real. She was way more relaxed. My heart soared; she was finally actually safe with a man.

She got happier and healthier quickly with him in her life. She could always be herself truthfully and safely with him, and he never let her down. She tells me she knows God always meant for him to be her dad. He's her natural medicine doctor, Dr Anthony Markus, and I see her after she sees him on Thursdays. Her eyes are full of light, and you can't wipe the smile off her face. We are all so happy to see her like this. It's about fucking time.

One Saturday night, it's just me and Kit hitting shooters. She loves to go and pick up straight girls and turn them half or completely gay and I like to watch. We always bet on how many numbers she can get. The police scold her many times for making out/hooking up with them in public; it doesn't stop her though.

This is mainly why we have girls following us around constantly.

This night we go in, there's heaps of people in the bar but it looks boring so we head back into the club part. The first thing I see is trouble: a guy we see out lots is getting picked on by two huge, hmmm, Serbians, maybe? 'Bella!' I say sternly, having been in a similar situation before. I go to grab her paw, but it's too fucking late. I hear this sweet, cheeky, girly voice yell,

'Oi, boys! How about you pick on someone your own size?'

I can't help but laugh at that. She's like an inch taller than me. Oh, fucking hell. Again? I really wish Holly were here! Hol would go up and back her up.

'What are you doing with my boyfriend?' Kit demands with attitude to the biggest guy. 'Go get us another drink, baby!' The guy doesn't seem to mind a tiny girl is saving him, doesn't waste a second and literally runs to the bar. The Serbians are looking her up and down. One of them spits, yes spits on the floor and says, 'You're about to get it, bitch.'

Kit, obviously amused, grins at him in a seriously daring fucking bring it dude kind of way. He starts cracking his knuckles, oh bloody fuck.

I take a deep breath, I know I'm gonna regret this, but I do it anyway. I step forward to back her up, tiny little me. I actually want to cry but I step up and say that she has backup. I don't know why it's so fucking embarrassing. The two men crack up with laughter; everyone who had gathered round laughs too. I feel like such a tool. I see Kit's mouth twitch and I want to disappear. I'm such an idiot, but the men are angrier now.

I swear I'm going to end up on the news: two tiny blondes killed by giant angry men in a club either tonight or another. I risk a glance at her. I feel like a fucking dick, like a dickhead not like I want sex …

I'm starting to have an anxiety attack. Thankfully, she sees it; she winks at me then puts her hands up in a T sign and calls a time out. 'Be right back, boys, she says, to smash your heads in…' She giggles, poking her tongue out at them cheekily. Then she swivels, whisks me up in her arms so fast with no warning and pushes her way through to the front door. She deposits me in the arms of Sven, her bouncer friend. Sven hugs me. 'You ok, kiddo?' I tell him the story with tears pouring down my face, I'm not strong like her.

I wonder if she's embarrassed of me and I melt into a full-blown anxiety attack. Sven wraps his arms around me and kisses my hair. It makes me uncomfortable. His hands start to wander and I want to scream for her but I don't. A little bit later I hear her yelling my name and she runs out of the club with blood pouring from her nose. 'Bunny? Bunny? BUNNY???' She's still yelling my name, even as she's looking right at me. She comes over and actually tears me from Sven's bit-too-tight grip.

She says thanks to him but she's giving him the evil eye. I ask her if she's ok. The bouncers get the attention of the Orchid Avenue police patrol. She's got her arms around me, telling me she's so proud of me, I'm sobbing that I'm a loser, and she's insisting that I'm wrong. Kissing my face and wiping blood all over me. Grosss.

Our moment is interrupted by police officer Darren yelling her name. Picture it for a second: a large crowd of people and a group of five big, strong, manly policemen and one of them suddenly starts looking around frantically and yelling the word 'Kitten?' over and over. It was pretty funny when you think about it. 'Yeah, babe?' she calls out, 'right here.'

She raises her paw so he can find us in the midst of the crowd that's surrounded and smothering her, asking what happened.

He rushes over, concerned when he sees blood. 'Oh, sweetness,' he coos, wiping away the blood with his fingers carefully—so disgusting (I hate blood). Then he wraps his arms around her. 'You're so silly, Angel,' he says. 'The hero, as always, but you're going to have to be more careful.' They are looking into each other's eyes intimately.

She leans forward, brushes her nose against his, and says 'sugar, I'm always going to help, but I'm ok.' He pulls her into a tight bear hug, his chin resting on her shoulder. He is holding her tight, but he is looking at me as he squeezes her hard. She is gripping him back and jealousy surges through me. I want to hold her; it's my turn. Tears drip down my cheeks again and he reaches out and bops my nose, saying, 'Oh, chook. You had a rough night too, huh?'

I nod sadly, so he sort of steps forward and pulls me into the hug. I'm stroking Kitten's back lovingly. With his free hand, he puts it in mine and squeezes.

I squeeze back and put my lips to his cheek in a little peck. 'Thank you,' I whisper, 'for caring about us.'

Kit politely excuses herself and runs over to the guy she saved. He doesn't let go; he holds me tight, and then he asks me out. I say yes a little too quick, but then add, 'If it's ok with Kit.' I give him my number and get lost in his eyes for a minute. When I look over, Kit is walking toward me. She's smiling the whole cab ride home and teases me gently. Another day in our wild random life.

She seems to attract trouble and weirdos, but if she ever needs it, she has a massive army of people who know her and probably have been saved by her to back her up.

Not that she needs it; she's perfectly capable of taking care of herself! Oh, BTW, the Russians (not Serbians, but I was close) didn't hit her in the face, obviously right, because she's too fast. She was apparently issuing a sharp roundhouse kick in the direction of the biggest one's head, as he was threateningly walking over to 'dismember her', when someone stepped forward out of the crowd, presumably to protect or stand by her. She head-butted their shoulder, ouch.

I do go on the date with the police officer; he's my first boyfriend. He is so sweet and understanding, such a gentleman, which Kit taught me, is really important. He opens the car door when he picks me up, kisses me on the cheek, and tells me I look lovely. We go to a seafood restaurant, I'm scared that I'm boring and plain next to my sex siren best friend, but he kisses me at the end and asks to see me again. I like him, but I know he really wants Kitten, and it's ok. At least I get some free dinners, I don't sleep with him though.

I don't know how someone who has been hurt so badly can be so loving.

I don't get how she can be so understanding and forgiving.

I can't work out how she can smile and be so kind and gentle, when she's been to hell.

It's impossible to tell how someone who spent so much time in darkness, can light up the world of everyone she meets.

I can't fathom how she stands up and fights for what's right and good when some people treat her so unkindly and all she's ever known is bad and evil.

How the fuck can someone so pure, sweet and beautiful endure, survive and overcome such evil?

How does her love, magic and light shine through all the darkness and dreadfulness she's experienced?

Out of the most disgusting, horrible, sad abuse story I've ever heard has come the most amazing person. She lived in hell; she survived and came back better. I feel like she was forged in the fires of Mt Doom herself.

The woman, the wonder, the legend: my friend, Kitten.

<u>Some quirky, interesting facts about my friend, Kitten:</u>

1. She hates pants. The first thing she will do when home is take off her pants, even before shoes, and if she doesn't have to go out, you can guarantee she is not wearing anything.

2. She is incredibly brave, will jump in front of a moving car or bullet to save someone. She will take on huge, strange men in clubs, and she will scale high dangerous things in the middle of the night drunk and sometimes fall off them. She will stand up for and do what's right always, no matter her opponent or any obstacle. But if something, even a little leaf, touches her in the water, she will squeal like a terrified three year old, get out super quickly and refuse to get back in. Once her own foot, numbed from the cold water touched her and she screamed loudly for like a whole minute. It nearly gave me a fucking heart attack. We laughed so hard and still tease her about it.

3. If she isn't melting chocolate to lick off naked women, she is absolutely useless in the kitchen. Can barely make toast.

4. She likes the Hanson song 'MMMBop'.

5. If you want to date/be with her, you better be chivalrous and charming, and you have to prove you're trustworthy and for real.

6. She has 5 songs written about her, by different bands that were recorded, put on CDs, on youtube etc. and sold worldwide.

7. She has a firewoman sex costume she's never used, so she works out in it; this is really sexy to watch, her working out in little shorts with suspenders.

8. She has over $5,000 worth of sexy lingerie.

9. She hates fishermen. She will yell at and lecture them if we walk past any, says it's barbaric torture. She's not wrong there though is she, really?

10. She hates the smell of butter. Cannot stand it.

11. If it's rainy or stormy, she will go out and dance naked in the rain. Hol always warns her about lightning, but Kitten insists the lightning would be too scared to hit her because it knows it'll get hurt. Yep, I have to agree with that one.

Chapter Two

Kitten

(This is the hard chapter. This is the tough part, guys.)

I don't know what it is, that you see, when you look at me

But you don't

You can't see me, but I see you

I see through it all to the very best of you

And I've fallen in love with what I see

I wish you could open your eyes and look at me

But you don't

You can't

You won't see me.

You will never be able to understand or even slightly comprehend the heaviness despair and massive pain that I feel. And nothing helps or lessens it; there are only temporary distractions. But still, I Kitten on (like soldier except me) through it all when I want to fall to my knees and scream and beg to die.

Every day is a fight to escape the horrible violent pain and fear filled memories, to try to repair the emotional and psychological damage, to ignore the sadness, a desperate struggle to keep the equilibrium within me so I don't allow myself to slip and be sucked into the black abyss, never to return, and also ignore the torment of watching the world around me:

Fall in love, get married, have children — things that are no longer meant for me. Instead, I run or go out, and I smile and laugh and pretend.

If I have written this right, you should be on your knees, with tears pouring down your face, your heart breaking for the little girl I once was and the horror and unfairness I was subjected to. At the same time, I hope you feel pride for the Kitten I have become and it's my greatest hope you feel inspired to be better, stronger and more grateful, to love harder and forgive harder.

To smile and love yourself, open your eyes and follow in my paw steps. Embrace and accept yourself. Work on yourself, be human and act like a mature adult, step up and help me change the world.

Don't cry for me; I'm already dead. Sadly, this is a true story; however, names, dates, places, and any other definitive information has been changed or omitted. I have looked into the eyes of the devil as he pushed sharp knives into my tiny little body and cut me inside. But I survived and grew up to be this amazing caring person. This is a story of triumph.

Heyaa, I'm Kitten. I am naughty, cheeky, kind and sweet. I smile brightly and laugh the loudest. I am crazy adventurous and wicked fun. I'm always inappropriate and I am the first person to step up and help in any situation. I am far more mature than people twenty, thirty years my senior but usually behave like a drunk 16 year old.

I am brave, affectionate and loving. I truly am these things, but the smile, laugh and happiness is a finely tuned act. I've been pretending to be ok most of my life. Under it all, I have a terrible secret. I have lived alone in the very depths of hell most of my life.

When I was little, I got used to pretending to be ok and thinking of lies to hide the truth about the cuts, bruises and blood in my undies, to protect my mummy from being murdered by bad men. The truth is I'm not ok, not even a little bit, never will be.

You can't undo the damage they did to me. I can't cry because they beat that out of me. I couldn't tell because they threatened to kill us and our families. I got so accustomed to pretending that it became second nature. I taught myself to not like food, attention or affection because I rarely got any or enough. Then I taught myself not to feel anything at all when I couldn't take the pain anymore and flew through the days not allowing myself to pause or think in case the darkness caught up with me. I pushed everyone away hard because I needed some semblance of control and safety.

Most of my life is a blur until this point. I have always been so desperate for attention, affection, love, acceptance and even acknowledgement. I don't really know how to feel real emotions like love, happiness and friendship, but I keep up the imitation. I am pretty sure I'm broken beyond repair.

I have always believed that love heals all and I hold a tiny shred of hope that one day, I'll meet someone who will love me enough to try to heal the shattered pieces of my heart/mind/soul and help me learn to enjoy friendship, intimacy and maybe even sex slowly.

One day when I was little, I realised I had to make a choice to try to find a way to be happy and have fun through all the horrible, unfair stuff in my life. So, despite all the bad stuff, I cultivated an unbreakable resolve to never let anything stop me having fun.

Most of my life, I believed one day I would grow up, I'd change the world; then I'd kill myself. I never allowed myself to hope or believe that anyone would love, want or even like me, or that things would get better. I was resigned to my fate. It would be sad for me; the little girl no one liked or wanted would grow up sad and alone and die alone. No one would notice or cry or even care.

I trained myself not to care what people thought, so it wouldn't hurt anymore when people hurt, mistreated or pushed me away and as a credit to my little self, I actually achieved this.

I never could work out what was so bad about me. I was just as sweet, caring and kind then as I am now. I acted my way through each day, but inside I was all sadness and despair. It was the only emotion I was comfortable with; the pain felt like home.

I used to hurt myself, it started as a punishment but then I realised I liked it, because I thought I deserved to be hurt and when I hurt myself first, I thought maybe it wouldn't hurt as much when other people hurt me. I completely closed myself off from real life and all emotion and went through life like a cold, unfeeling robot.

Most little girls dream of being mums; I dreamt of killing myself so no one could hurt me ever again, and I made that promise to myself. I did try several times to commit suicide. Each time I woke up in hospital filled with despair that I was still alive. I didn't want to be here. I didn't want to hurt anymore, to remember and be constantly running from and fighting the darkness.

I won't lie to you, this is not going to be the easiest chapter to read because I'm going to be incredibly brave and completely honest and open about what happened to me, how it affected me then, growing up and how it still affects me today. There are things in here that will shake you to your very core. There are side effects of child sex abuse that people don't understand and don't want to think or talk about. I believe it's important to educate everyone on this, so I'm being bold and completely honest.

But don't worry I get my happy ending. After all that time alone in the darkness, I meet a woman, Holly, who loves me and fights for me.

She starts to rebuild my shattered psyche and then later, I meet a few men that I can actually trust, and one day I meet an incredibly sexy fireman who holds the key and shows me I can feel sexual pleasure; a great man, my knight in shining armour, who wakes me up emotionally! (A boy! WOW didn't think that would ever happen!) I rise above it all, and one day I smile real smiles, laugh genuinely and am truly happy. I hope by the end of reading this, you understand.

I'm scared you'll hate me though, but as embarrassing, shameful and disgusting as parts of this book are, they are so very important. There are other little girls and boys out there who were hurt like I was and now they are struggling, hurting adults and this book will help them. This has been so hard for me to write, it almost crushed me and cost me my sanity, but if it saves or changes even one life, it's worth it. Although, I have no doubt it will change/help and save many lives. Ok, deep breath, guys. Here it comes. The cold, hard, horrible truth about child sex abuse.

There are things in this world that are truly unfathomably horrific, and no one should have to experience them, let alone a small child. Although there will never be justice for me, I take comfort in knowing that this book will help many others who have been hurt in many ways and will educate people on how to help them (I will do a special chapter on recognising and supporting people who have been through intense trauma). I am an incredibly successful private counsellor now specialising in trauma.

At the end of this book, you will find an email address, and if you have been hurt and you are falling, please email me; I will catch you. I know. Trust me...

I KNOW.

Here is my story:

Oodles of love

Always & forever,

Kitten.

Before I start, let's talk about the cycle of abuse. Which very simply explained means someone hurts, abuses or neglects someone else because they were hurt, abused or neglected first. This of course does not give them the right to be abusive, but once you have been abused, if no one helps you after and if you don't process the trauma properly, something breaks inside you. It really isn't their fault; they can't help it because they don't know any better. It stunts and deforms natural emotional growth and development.

I am not affected by the cycle. I have the purest heart and would not hurt any living creature, but I need you to understand that my mum wasn't loving or affectionate towards me because her parents didn't treat her properly. They were cruel and unloving, and it is no fault of hers or her parents'. The abuse began generations ago. (This can be described /defined as generational trauma.) Years later, mum and I grow very close, and I help her heal her trauma wounds/scars.

I know it's going to be really hard for you to understand, but the same goes for the men who hurt me. They are just as much victims as I was, but no one ever helped them, and their pain will never be acknowledged because they are now perpetrators.

I can't even bear to let myself think about what truly unspeakable depravity and terror that poor man must have been subjected to, to be able to rape and torture his own daughter and force his son to rape his little sister. All I feel is compassion and empathy. No one will ever care about his torment.

This is what happens when things like abuse or traumatic experiences are not properly treated: the human psyche begins to twist and splinter in an effort to escape the pain and trauma. Consequently, you end up with a confused person in deep pain with a fractured personality. This is how murderers, abusers and psychopaths/sociopaths are born. Also how PTSD begins.

Don't get me wrong, I am full of white-hot anger for the pain I was forced to endure, not just physical but mental and emotional. I have nightmares of little girls screaming in pain as men cut them inside with sharp knives and other horrible things. We weren't allowed to scream or cry, but in my dreams, we all scream nail-curling, mind-boggling screams of pain and we bawl our little eyes out.

I have anger for the darkness and memories that haunt my every step and the nightmares that leave me shaking and wishing for heaven. (I have been too afraid to sleep most of my life.) But mostly anger for my ruined life and the parts of life I missed out on ... love, happiness, friendship, the chance to have a family. I had to shut my heart and feelings down and off in order to survive it all.

However, they are just as worthy of your understanding and sympathy as I am. Not that I am in any way condoning their behaviour, of course. Amy once asked me what I'd do/say if I ever met them as an adult, and I replied that I'd take them in my arms and hug them, then I'd counsel and help them. Because as angry as I am, I understand that they were hurt first and are still alone and hurting and because of that, plus my in-depth understanding of human intellect, emotions and behaviours, I understand and would help them. Not an easy decision, trust me!

So, I guess I'll start at the beginning: at home.

I remember always being alone. I'm incredibly smart, mature, and perceptive, and from a very young age, I had an adult consciousness. I would entertain myself with deep thoughts about life and relationships. No one, not even my mum, ever played with me, touched, held me nor gave me any loving affection or attention. Mum barely even looked at me, and if she did, it wasn't in a loving way; it was in anger. She used to bully and make fun of me in front of and with her friends, while I was there, it wasn't fair; I was too small to stick up for myself so I just stood there trying not to cry while they all laughed at me.

She was always so mean to me, once I asked her if we could sit together while we watched a movie and she said no, so she sat on her lounge and I sat alone, in my chair, not really watching the movie but wondering if I just got up and left, just walked out into the night, never to be seen again, if she'd even notice. She'd probably be happy she didn't have to see me ever again.

I started writing when I was about 3. Not actual writing, but stories in my head. My piece-of-crap father left when I was tiny, so my mum worked hard to provide for us. We stayed with my grandmother when I was very small. My mum was always yelling at and angry with me.

My nanna would say, 'Come to your nanna,' and I would run into her arms a bundle of snot and tears. I could see quite clearly that my mum did not like me. For a small child, this was utterly heartbreaking. I felt so desperately sad, alone, heartbroken, worthless, not enough. I thought I must be so hideous, horrible and disgusting!

When I was 5, Mum bought us a house. We moved away and she worked harder than ever - I rarely saw her. When I did, she was even more tired and angry. I could never do anything right and whenever I corrected a behaviour that upset her, two more would pop up. All she did was scream at me. I could never keep up or please her. I was constantly writing her letters of apology, but it was never enough. I tried so hard, but it was never enough. No one liked, cared about or wanted me. I was unloved and alone.

My mum was commuting 2.5 hours a day to work to provide for us. She was always frustrated and angry. She barely fed me and even when she did, it was junk like McDonalds which sounds like every kid's dream, but it's not when it's all you get. Then she would get angry at me for eating it so quickly. I was always starving, because I didn't get much to eat.

I used to take my coloured pencils into her room in the early mornings on the weekends and colour next to her bed while she slept, just to be near her when she wasn't angry and yelling at me.

I would watch TV and study human relationships and interactions. I had no real human relationships to compare it to, so it was really hard for me in social situations. I amused myself by taking each scenario and going through as many possible variations to each situation as possible. People were always commenting that I was an old soul, on the odd occasion Mum took me to the supermarket with her.

One day I'm riding my bike in our street, going down the hill fast. As I pass our house, my mum steps outside and I meet her eye and smile, lifting one hand off the handlebars to wave. She meets my gaze and looks away instantly, as if horrified she'd looked at me. It makes me sad and embarrassed. I stack my bike bad, flying over the handlebars and really hurting myself, crying out loudly in pain as I hit and skid along the bitumen. I lie there bleeding and in so much pain for ages. I don't let myself cry because I want my mummy to be proud of me for being brave when she comes to help me.

I lie there for hours, but she never comes. I think at least one of my neighbours might come and help me. No one comes; no one cares.

I'm in so much pain and bleeding heavily. I can feel my foot and ankle swelling up. Eventually, it starts to get dark, and someone drives into the street. My heart lightens with hope, surely they will come and help me, maybe no one came because they are out.

They stop to move my bike out of the way. They don't help me up or ask if I'm ok. They drive up onto the neighbours' lawn and drive around me! However, in that exact second, I realise as tears pour down my little cheeks, I am completely unwanted and alone and it all has to come from me. As I lie in the street bleeding, with badly torn ligaments in my ankle, I realise no one is ever going to care. I'm going to be alone and unwanted forever.

So, I get up, finding it far too painful to even try to put weight on my foot, hop over to my bike, pick it up, and hop my way home dragging it behind me. When I get there, Mum screams at me for treating my bike in such a way and threatens to never buy me anything expensive ever again.

When I finally get inside (after hopping up a curb and over a yard, dragging a bike, then up three stairs), utterly exhausted, I hop my way to the tissues. Being too small to open a band aid and in too much pain to hop to the bathroom, I just hold the tissues on the gashes on my arms and legs until it stops bleeding. I don't get any dinner and am awake all night in pain, crying and starving.

However, as much as it hurt my feelings and broke my little heart, in this event, I realised I was invincible and I didn't need anyone. If no one liked or wanted me, fine, I'd take care of myself and have fun alone. I knew there was nothing wrong with my behaviour. I was polite and always offered to help, I was well behaved, and I just looked like a regular kid. I gave up trying to work out what was wrong with me, why everyone was always so mean and nasty, and stopped caring what everyone else thought.

A few months after this, the paedophile ring abuse started. I had absolutely no male influences in my young life. No brother, cousin, grandfather that was around. No idea of how men should behave around little girls.

Ok, steel yourself guys. The next bit isn't fun and I can't think of a way to soften it, sorry, although I did try, but it's really important this is in here. It's only my chapter though. There are only a few pages of this really hard stuff; then it gets very interesting again.

There was a little girl who lived across the street. She had an older teenage brother. I was not very good at playing with kids, having always played alone and amused myself with adult ponderings, but I tried to pretend to be a child. When we were playing with other kids in the street, she would always tell us dirty stories. The other kids and I would sit and listen, perplexed and fascinated. It wasn't until I started writing this book that I realised her stories were true; those were things they did to her, and they did some of them to me too. Her father had lots of male friends, and it was fun when they came over, at first.

They would spin us around by our arms and legs and throw us in the air. I loved those moments. I felt like I was part of a family and couldn't get enough.

One day, her father called me out into the back room. It had a strange set-up with beds, tables and rope, but I failed to really notice this that first day. I was thrilled to be getting some attention. I also didn't notice his pants were not on properly until he invited me to sit on his lap. Then I saw his thing, I turned to run away, but he grabbed my arm, yanked me back, and yelled at me to pull my pants down. I had never had a man want to be alone with me before, and it was the first time a man had yelled at me. I was shocked and confused.

I did what he said; then he pulled me onto his lap and started touching me between my legs. I knew I wasn't supposed to be touched there, but I didn't really understand what he was doing, only that it was wrong. It made me feel yucky, and I wanted him to stop. I started to say, 'Don't,' but he spoke over the top of me, saying, 'Do you like that? That feels nice, doesn't it?' Inside, panic started to overcome me. If I said no, would he yell at me again? Would I get in trouble?

Would he say I wasn't allowed to come over anymore or play with his daughter (my only friend)? Would he tell my mum?

Would she hate me even more?

Would I go back to being completely alone again?

This is where for most of my life, I believed it was my fault: that I invited it because I said yes even though I didn't like it, because I was trying to run every scenario and option through my head quickly and I was confused and scared. He was touching me harder, and it felt so strange and uncomfortable I eventually said yes, hoping he would stop it. He said that I was a good girl and lifted me up, pushing me down onto his thingy. It hurt so much, and everything was moving in slow motion. I didn't know what was happening or how to stop it.

I wanted to scream, but I couldn't seem to make any sound other than a whimper. He pushed me up and down over and over, then grunted and moaned, put me down, and told me to pull my pants up. There was some gross, sticky stuff between my legs. I thought it was from me, that maybe I was sick (maybe this why no one liked me?)I ran away, shocked and disgusted.

Little did I know it was going to get so much worse. I didn't even think to tell my mum because I had no male behaviour to compare it to and I wasn't sure what had actually happened. For all my great intellect, it left me stumped. I'd seen a few sex scenes on TV, but they were different. Also, I was scared she'd say I wasn't allowed to play there anymore; then I'd go back to being alone always.

Life went on as it always did. Things at home became worse. Mum started blaming me for things no small child could possibly do. Even though I was confused about what happened, I still spent as much time as possible at the neighbour's house. Some of the time, it was fun. There was another little girl who would play with us. We'd eat ice blocks and run through the sprinklers. One day, all of her father's friends came over all at once. It was a hot summer day. I remember the warm smell of the grass and flowers on the breeze.

Normally, it was three or four at a time, and sometimes they would take the other little girls away for some secret playtime that I was left out of. In my head, I imagined cakes and lollies and toys. (But that was clearly only for non-hideous little girls; I was left out again.)

It was fun at first, the men giving us attention and playing with us. Then I noticed they had all gone quiet. All of a sudden, on some secret adult cue that went over my head, they grabbed all three of us and took us out in the back room. I was confused and scared. I vaguely remember Annie pleading with her dad. 'Daddy, no. Please, no.'

The back room looked a little different. There were all these things like cutlery and instruments / tools set out on one table, the beds and other tables had more ropes. It seemed like all of a sudden, the men were all naked, and so were the other girls. Then they took my clothes off me. I was desperately confused. I could not even slightly comprehend the gravity of what was about to happen, but

I was beyond terrified. I remembered what he'd done to me a few weeks ago and felt so sick with fear. This was not the happy, fun secret playtime I imagined.

I saw one of the men tying Helen's legs open and started to scream. I was swiftly hit in the face by a fist, with the full force of an adult male punching a tiny almost 6 year old girl directly in the face. No screaming, no crying and if I ever told anyone, they would kill us and our mums. Then the real horror began.

I looked at Annie, and she had embarrassment and some unreadable expression of horror on her face as her father pushed her legs open, up in the air then behind her ears, and raped her right in front of her best friend. I was so confused, is that what happened in real families? They did truly horrible things to us in those sessions.

They would rape us; force us to watch and sometimes orgasm as the other girls were raped. They would use tools and instruments on us, including sharp knives. I clearly remember the feel of cold metal or steel (like the smaller end of a spanner or wrench I think) inside me and hard biting plastic. The feeling of a sharp knife slicing and puncturing me inside. We had to do terrible things to them, to ourselves and worst, to the other girls sometimes. I realised fairly quickly if you braced yourself when they put it in, it didn't hurt as bad.

Then I'd talk to myself in my head, telling myself that it would be over soon and that I was ok, which I did when mum was really angry and yelling. Then I'd count, it did help. I tried to explain to the other little girls that you brace yourself, and then think of other things. They stared at me blankly like I'd just started speaking Russian.

I hated to watch them hurt the other girls; they seemed so little and childish. After talking to them didn't work, I tried to beg the men not to hurt them. They thought it was hilarious, taunted me and threw a brick at my face, telling me to shut up. I still have the scar on my forehead where it hit me. Then I tried to break free so I could physically try to stop them.

I got a serious beating. One day, I was forced to watch as 'Uncle' Peter raped both the other girls. They made us call Annie's dad 'Dad' and the other men 'uncle'. Some of the men lived in or near my street. They used to tie us down so tightly we could barely move. My body would spasm upwards with the pain and shock, and every tiny flinch in the tight binds hurt a lot. The constant back and forth movement with force as they raped me sometimes left rope burns on my wrists and ankles.

Uncle Peter was always so rough. I watched their little bodies jolt in pain, the silent tears they couldn't fight and the looks of pain and despair on their faces. I had to do something. I went through the unfairly short list of possibilities in my mind. I was distracted by it being 'my turn', as Peter said jollily. I briefly met the tear-filled, pain-stricken eyes of the other girls. Then I took a deep breath, bit my lip, and prepared myself for the pain I knew was coming. He was saying, 'Yeah, you like that, don't you? That feels good, doesn't it?'

And then he ordered me to tell him I wanted 'IT'.

Still unsure exactly what IT was that they were doing to me, and with no other option, I complied, but I realised they always said the same things to all of us, and it hit me. If I said what they wanted me to and actually pretended to like it, maybe they would hurt me instead of the other girls. I didn't consider enough what that would mean for me. But the next time the whole lot of them turned up, I was ready.

When Peter went to grab Helen, I said, 'No, Uncle Peter. I want it, I like it.' I was so thrilled that it worked until he slammed into me. That day, I was raped by five different men, numerous times.

By the end of it, I couldn't walk properly and blood was dripping down my legs. Maybe running is a better adjective. Annie's mum would stitch us up herself, with no anaesthetic and when our clothes got really bloody, she would wash them and we'd be sent home in old ones telling our mums we 'had an accident.'

That she was washing them. I repeat, if the damage was really bad, she would stitch us up herself, with no anaesthetic. Sewing needle and thread.

After our little bodies had been badly torn and injured, excruciating isn't even close. When I was small, I couldn't understand how she could let them do those things to us. She knew we were in pain; she cleaned up the blood, gave us stitches, lied to our mums. However, as an adult I realise she was a prisoner of that monster. Probably suffered similar things herself. The pain barely bothered me; I was jubilant that I finally outwitted the morons.

I knew I was smarter than them, but often anxiety and fear worked me into a frantic panic and rendered me unable to think straight and running in literal circles as I tried to escape their evil clutches.

So, it was great to finally win, and more importantly I'd saved the other girls from all that pain. I guess, because of my intellect and maturity I felt the need to protect them as I still do with absolutely everyone. Looking back, I'm proud of my sacrifice but sad I brought so much hurt onto my poor, sweet little self. The men passed me around like I meant nothing.

This mirrored how I felt. Unimportant, unloved, nothing. That was me. I thought the other girls would thank me, and it broke my heart when they didn't.

One spring day, I looked out the window to see three men marching across the road to get me. Realistically, I could have run out the back door and down onto the street to another neighbour. But I flipped. I was still sore from the last session and anxiety and terror tore through me. I wanted to cry, to disappear, and I ran around my house in circles in a frantic panic. I could have even locked myself in the toilet, but I couldn't force myself to calm enough to think. I ran through the double-entry bathroom into my mum's room, then through the lounge room and saw they were on my lawn.

I tore back through the bathroom and repeated this until I felt strong hands grab me. I briefly glimpsed an open window and the grass of my backyard before I went limp with exhaustion and defeat.

They grabbed some knives out of my kitchen drawer and a few other torture items before we left. I have nightmares of this day for most of my life.

I always tried really hard not to look at or see what scary tool, knife, bike tyre pump, utensil, or other terrifying thing they were going to hurt me with, because it always came back to me in my nightmares and it still does.

One day at school, the teacher gave us a talk about inappropriate behaviour and said to tell them if anyone was bothering us. I had an idea, maybe if I said something, they would realise something was very wrong and help me. So, I made up a story that an older boy would wait for me at the gate. She told my mum and they tried to get more info out of me, but I had none. I wasn't allowed to tell the truth.

Then one day the teacher told me they'd been watching after school and knew I was lying. 'But, but, but,' I spluttered, trying desperately to find words to subtly let her know I was being hurt, but she turned mean.

'You're a liar, you little shit! You've been wasting our time. Admit you're lying, you disgusting little pig.' She had her face so close to mine she was spitting on me as she yelled. Despair filled my body.

My tiny shred of hope was crushed. Seeing no other option, I slumped in sad defeat and said I was lying.

I felt so frustrated and disappointed I wet myself and was so embarrassed. I slid off the chair onto the floor and just wished for it to end. She then yelled at me for wetting myself. I just wanted to be gone.

In retrospect, I must have had a UTI because I didn't wet myself, even though it is a common side effect of sexual abuse. NB: it's usually consistent bedwetting, especially in older children. It can be a dead giveaway, any child above seven or eight — but not always; some children have this problem for other psychological/ emotional reasons!

I hated adults. They were always yelling at me. It seemed like no one was going to help me. I guess eventually those men would hurt me so bad they'd kill me. I hoped that was soon. I felt bad for my mummy. She'd be alone, but she didn't like me anyway.

Maybe she could get a new kid, one she actually liked and wanted … knowing she didn't want me made me feel very very sad and alone. I was good, always tried to help, was always polite, well behaved but nothing was ever enough. I never got any attention or affection or even acknowledgment from her.

I must have something so truly terrible and disgusting about me, if not even my own mummy could stand me.

I can clearly remember the frustration I felt, knowing I was so very smart but being unable to find a way out. As an adult, I realise there was no way out. They were horrible monsters who did terrible, unspeakable things to little girls for fun. I am 100% sure they would be capable of murder.

Sometimes they would make us take off our clothes and parade us around naked so they could choose which little girl they wanted, making us do things like bend over and stuff. It was so embarrassing. It was horrible because even though I didn't want to get chosen, it made me feel even worse about myself and embarrassed if I got picked last. I was usually picked first though.

Guys, reeeaaally baad stuff coming, but it's short and it's the last of the abuse stuff.

My mum decided to take a holiday, and she sent me to stay at the neighbour's. She bought me this pink hard plastic toothbrush case, one of the big old-skool ones, about 3 cm wide.

It was a nightmare; I barely slept the entire time, I was so afraid. One day we had another session with all nine of the men.

Peter was in a really bad mood and he was pushing his thingy so far down my throat I kept almost puking. I tried so hard not to, because he whipped me with his belt, buckle and all last time I puked. Anyway, as I had his thing in my mouth, I couldn't save the other girls, and the other men were being really rough too. He shoved my head down hard and my teeth slipped a little bit. He smacked the back of my head and yelled at me. The slap caused it to go further in quickly with force, it hurt so bad and I puked. I couldn't stop it. He yelled that I was a disgusting slut and made me keep going. I kept retching. The smell of vomit was disgusting. I could taste it. I couldn't breathe properly. It was disgusting and horrible, stinging my eyes and nose. I couldn't stop gagging. It felt like my throat was tearing with him in there and my gagging.

I'd just thrown up the first decent meal I'd had in a week, so back to really bad empty belly pain. It was so unfair. I could see other girls were being badly hurt and I snapped. Having always been a rebel, I let my teeth slip properly, dragging them down his thing till I tasted blood. He was furious. He ripped my head up by my hair so hard I was sure he'd snapped my neck.

He flipped me over and ploughed into me hard as he could. It was so fast, I didn't have a chance to brace myself, and I accidentally screamed in pain. He back handed me hard. Since he'd let go of one of my legs, I kicked him as hard as I could in the face.

I was triumphant for a few seconds until I saw him pick up my toothbrush case, which I hadn't seen until then. Heavy terrified black despair engulfed me. I knew what was next. I guess though, since he already had it, he was planning on using it, even before my rebellious behaviour had happened.

All of a sudden I was being held down and he slammed it into me over and over. I can't even begin to describe the pain. I could feel the damage, my skin tearing painfully, blood spraying and running all over my butt and thighs. I could feel the impact and pain of every single blow right up in my stomach and chest. It was unbearable.

I was sure it would kill me. I told myself in my head over and over that it would be ok, that I'd die in a second and it would be over. It seemed to go forever and anxiety tore through my whole body. It was so unbelievably horrible, scary and painful. But I didn't die; the level of pain was about 600. Eventually the other men had to restrain him. I saw the case as he set it down; it was covered in bits of my skin and dripping blood. Peter had my blood almost up to his elbows. I was in so much pain and he'd done so much damage. I waited and hoped to die.

I don't know how I didn't die actually. Going to the bathroom was excruciating. Walking, every tiny movement, even breathing caused unbearable pain. I bled for ages after. I remember her mum stitching and washing the area with something. It stung so badly on top of the pain I already had from the damage! I literally tried to will myself to die. I thought about jumping in front of a car to end my life, but I couldn't do that because it would probably hurt someone else.

I was starting to think about running away for real. I couldn't take it anymore; it was getting worse. But Mum was home beginning of next week, and then at least it wouldn't be constant.

I just wanted to die.

A few days after this, her older teenage brother took me to the store to get some stuff. He normally only hurt us when the older men made him, but today he hurt me all on his own. Thankfully in my butt, but it was still excruciating. My mum came home a few days later. Weeks later at dinner one night, I mentioned that a sausage resembled Jim (the son's) doodle. Finally, finally, finally Mum realised something was up. I couldn't tell about the older men, but the police came when Mum made a big fuss about the teenage boy hurting me. She only knew about the boy.

Once my eyes had started watering from the pain, I tried so hard but I couldn't stop it. I knew I was in trouble. I have a very cheeky, rebellious personality and they seemed to take any slight slip as an excuse to beat me. Sometimes two or three of them would take turns torturing me. I remember being thrown across a room with such force I flew through the air for what seemed like ten minutes, my arms and legs flailing, but I made sure my face was emotionless. Christmas trees are nice to look at, but being thrown and landing in one isn't much fun. Then I got into trouble for breaking the ornaments.

I always tried so hard not to cry or scream or be sick or do anything wrong. I think sometimes they just beat me for fun. Those men raped me over 40 times. It went on for almost two long terrifying years. I spend many years after this secretly thinking; maybe the only thing I'm good for is to be used by men like this. Honestly there is a part of me that still occasionally thinks all I'm good for is sex. Ok, phew!

That's the end of the really nasty, disturbing abuse stuff I'm sorry you had to read that. I hope you're ok! Don't worry; it's an easier read now.

Mum sent me to after school care when I was 8. I actually made some friends. One afternoon, I fell off the play equipment and hurt my wrist. The supervisors wanted to take me to the doctor, a male doctor. I remembered the last time I was alone with a man and I got upset, refusing to go. They chased me around the yard, and I assumed it was some plot to hurt me again and they were in on it. (Why else would they be so persistent?) I have a full-blown melt down, crying and yelling for my mum. The 3 adult women were nasty, laughing at me and saying things like, 'can you believe this crap? This is ridiculous … like a 3 year old.'

I stood there, terrified and trembling with fear while the other kids backed away and stared at me. I knew that was the end of my friendships. Frustrated water started to well in my eyes and I thought, oh no, now they will beat me, and then they will probably make me see the man who would hurt me again. I stood there, all barely 4 feet of me, desperately wishing I were dead so I didn't have to go through this again.

Then I just ran, I was so embarrassed and so sad about losing my new friends, plus they still wanted me to see the doctor. There was no other option; I took off out the door and onto the streets. I ran across a four-lane road to the deserted, dark school and sat hiding in bushes, waiting till

I saw Mum's car. It wasn't fair. I was cold and hungry. They usually gave us a snack, and I was missing out on food!!

I have no idea what the hell was wrong with those women or anyone else who can't discern from this sort of behaviour that I'd been through trauma. Most bad/strange behaviour stems from trauma, and if it's untreated and not met with patience, love and understanding, it spirals and gets worse; in severe cases becoming a psychological pathology or even psychosis.

It's this sort of thing that creates serial killers, etc. HELP HURTING PEOPLE, you can't expect people to behave rationally or recognise their behaviour if you don't help them first.

Be gentle and loving: listening, caring, talking, hugging, distracting, being friendly, including them and helping them through the tough times. This is how we heal everyone. Behaving like mature adults and recognising why people behave/act/speak the way they do. Reading between the lines. For more info, refer to the bonus counselling chapter.

When I was 10, I saw a proper sex scene and realised it was sex they were doing. I was still a little too young to be able to objectively apply the concept of rape to my experiences. Around this time, I started hanging out with older kids, partly because I could communicate with them more easily; they seemed to like me and think I was fun and funny, but also because I'd overheard them talking about sex and I needed more info. However, when I tried to join in the conversations about naughty things boys and girls do, they turned on me, their eyes narrowing into slits and looking at me then treating me like a disgusting piece of trash.

I was so confused and broken hearted ... still not realising that dads didn't usually do that to their daughters.

One day, when I'm 11, mum takes me to the doctor to have a mole removed, he is male and I don't want to be alone with him, mum tries to push me telling me I'm being silly. I refuse and he takes my hand and tries to lead me away. In retrospect he was probably trying to be kind, but I was terrified so I throw a loud, messy tantrum.

Mum comes into the treatment area, the doctor starts lasering off the mole, but even after it's gone, he keeps burning into my hand, I'm screaming in pain, mum watches and doesn't protest just stands there and lets him burn a hole the size of a 5cent piece into my little hand. I guess I must have embarrassed him with my loud tantrum and refusing to be alone with him in the waiting room. Why else would he do that? Why? I couldn't even cry. By this point I'd taught myself not to feel anymore, so I just sat there and endured it, emotionlessly. Talking to myself in my head. This experience is what gives me the idea to burn myself as punishment.

I tried my best to push through life. I couldn't do anything right. When I was 12, my school friends started talking about masturbation. I was so confused and also disgusted, but after a while I wanted to be able to join in talking about it, so I tried touching myself.

It was supposed to feel good. I couldn't feel a thing other than horror and disgust. I felt so ashamed I got a lighter and burnt a hole in my leg. I watched in fascination as the skin shrivelled and turned white as I burnt it. It hurt like hell, but I needed to distance myself from the emotional pain and I had to punish myself for trying to like it even though I was numb. When I was little, I trained it out of myself because it was too confusing and unfair. They were adult males; they knew how to stimulate and manipulate a girl's/woman's body. The human body can feel and respond to pleasure from a young age.

Even though I didn't understand and definitely did not like/enjoy/want any of it, my body was stimulated, manipulated and forced to orgasm over and over against my will. Just to be completely clear here, I did not feel any pleasure but connected and deduced from the things they said it was supposed to be like that. There was nothing I could do to stop my body responding in that way. I eventually sort of, not completely, retrained myself to respond to pleasure as a young adult — I actually trained my body not to feel pleasure when touched that way or any way at all.

But it was difficult to fight the feelings of revulsion and shame. It took me years to retrain myself and once I got to the point I could make myself come, I went through a phase where I did it heaps, which I suppose is true of most people. But I would beat up, berate and often cut or burn myself afterwards. I felt so ashamed and so much self-loathing over something that should have been completely natural and a normal learning experience. How disgusting was I to do that to myself after what happened with those men.

Then my friends started getting boyfriends. I was popular with the boys and dated a couple but hated them touching me, which didn't go over too well with teenage boys, hehe. I was busy trying to keep myself together and failing. The pressure was starting to show now I'd hit puberty. I hated the way boys and men looked at me and I tried to hide my sexuality.

I would terrorise my male teachers with my outlandish behaviour. Not sexual, just class clown with wicked bad attitude kind of thing. I was getting attention from boys and men everywhere and hated it.

Everyone always misunderstood my intentions (and often still do). I'm cheeky, naughty and flirty always, and I'm friendly, affectionate and caring. Men think I'm interested and that it's some sort of an invitation. I'm not/it's not ever. I only want boys as friends.

High school got hard because my friends' older brothers and sometimes fathers were showing me attention and climbing into bed with me at sleepovers. Older boys were always making me do sexual stuff I didn't want to do. I had one 'friend' who clearly was not my friend, but I always put up with more than I should have because I was still desperate for attention affection and acceptance. She was in the room a couple of times when her older brother and his friends hurt me. I remember her laughing. I was 14.

They did horrible things. Not just sex stuff, they would torture me too. It made me angry, but I was a teenager, and it was difficult to make best friends.

So I started hanging with the older kids, which was so much easier for me, and got invited to their parties, which was Kool. I still had friends in my year and went to those parties too. As always, I was the life of the party (and I still am).

Still, the darkness chased my every step, hovering threateningly and taunting me, always trying to steal me away. So I did my little robot act to get through the days, not learning or paying any attention. I started to feel anger towards my mum. Why didn't she protect me? I know as an adult that she couldn't have known. Except for the blood in my undies thing, but I always told her I fell on my bike or something and hurt myself that way. How could she not see through that FFS! Also, I washed and dressed myself from a young age, so maybe she never actually saw the damage.

I guess I had to lie convincingly enough to protect her - I hope that's what. But even now thinking about it, I feel sadness, disappointment and anger. If you love someone enough, you can feel when they are hurting like Holly does, she can feel me slipping even before I fall. More proof Mum didn't love me. Not that any further evidence was needed; part of me sadly suspects she knew, though.

When I'm 15, things start to slip. I start drinking to get through the days. I was always alone. Don't get me wrong, I had friends, but I was still alone with the memories and my pain.

The girl I am today is what I built when I crawled my way out of the depths of hell from darkness, from nothingness. Holly is right; I am incredible and strong, smart, fierce, brave, kind, loving, plus naughty, cheeky, etc, but I taught myself how to dress myself, tie my shoelaces, etc. I still can't cook. I tried to make pancakes out of those premix bottles once and I got it everywhere: On the wall, in my hair (how?!!!!?), all over the floor. I ended up eating half-cooked, yet somehow still burnt, pancake batter, but I digress.

By the time I'm 17, it all gets too much. I'm sleeping at my best friend Mary's more than I am at home because I'm so angry with my mum and myself. I start to lose my grip big time. I need people to see I'm hurting so bad, yet I can't say the truth, so I think of a lie. I tell my friends that I was sick and probably going to die. I am and always have been in perfect health, but it wasn't too far off the truth - I was planning on killing myself. They are very caring and sweet and tears are shed. About three years later I tell them the truth and they are understanding.

I was so desperate for someone to see how badly I was hurting. I'm so ashamed I lied to them though. No one had ever offered to help me. Even after Mum thought it was just the teenage boy who raped me, no one ever offered me counselling or anything. I was alone with it all for all those years.

I am so embarrassed that I lied. I saw no other choice. This is the last lie I tell. Well, to be honest, I have to lie sometimes to get myself out of trouble, usually with police. 'No, officer, that wasn't me climbing that...I swear!' But unless a lie is a necessity, I can't do it. I go all red, my voice goes squeaky like my balls are dropping and I stutter.

I guess having to spend most of my young life lying was enough. I feel like you must think I'm disgusting, deplorable and horrible and I completely understand. I felt that way about myself most of my life. Except now I know it's normal, not my fault or in my control.

When I was in my late teens, I started researching this and although I never did find an abuse story anywhere near as horrific as my own, I did find that many women and men had the same problems growing up after abuse. Some with worse problems I didn't have, like masturbating furiously in your sleep or apparently at other times. So if you have this problem, it's normal too. Waking up or being aroused after thoughts or dreams of this nature is also normal. Disgusting and horrible but still entirely normal. Not within your control.

There are many side effects from a shattered psyche after sexual (or other) abuse and NONE OF THIS is your fault or under your control. Once you realise this, the burden becomes a bit lighter. Just try to train bad behaviours out of yourself.

Mortifying example: I went through a stage in the beginning where I couldn't feel pleasure or come unless I was thinking about those men hurting me. It was reprehensible.

I hated myself; it was disgusting. I didn't want to do it, don't misunderstand me, but I just sort of needed to. This happens often with sex abuse victims, especially if it happened when you were young. Often, I'd hurt myself as punishment right after. But I couldn't control it, so I trained it out slowly. First, I imagined myself older being hurt, then the men younger, and I eventually got to the point where I could come imagining a boy my own age forcing me. Then I made it less violent, like we were joking around. Eventually I got to the point where I just thought about him being a bit rough but not forcing me, then just making love. I did it; I won. Gooo, Kitten! This was my first and biggest victory.

This comes back to me sometimes as a grown up, and I use the same techniques. My healing journey has only really begun. One day, I'll find a way to stamp out/overcome all these unfair problems and behaviours.

When I was a teenager, like 16–19, I kind of made myself have boyfriends to at least try to be normal. It was a nightmare. The first one's dad kissed me one night when we were out at a club, then tried to play footsy with me under the table at family dinners.

His mum eyed me like she was disgusted and furious with me. I sat there terrified into stone. But I did not encourage it at all. His dad tried to drug me at a club one night and I was done.

The second one was my only semi-serious relationship. He got my name tattooed on him after we'd been dating a month; then he started yelling at and trying to control me. He often pushed and manipulated me into sex, then refused to use condoms, despite my protests.

He got me pregnant, which was a miracle, and I was so excited. I had names picked out: Estella, or Stella for short, or Graciella for a girl and Ji or Raphael for a boy. I'd decide when I met them. I was so excited. It was a dream come true. My miracle baby. I was so happy, was determined to be the best mum ever! Then the father turned really mean and violent, constantly screaming at me, hiding my things, threatening me, being even more controlling, refusing to let me go out with my friends.

My heart broke yet again. This man was going to be violent and a wife beater. My hope shattered, I thought of my childhood and how Annie's mum looked after she'd be beaten up. I could not bring a child into an unstable environment. No matter how desperately I wanted my baby, I would not bring a child into an abusive family situation.

I wanted so badly to be selfish, but I couldn't and honestly, as badly as it hurt then and still deeply hurts me today to give up my child and my one chance to be a mum, I don't regret it.

It would have been wrong, unforgivable, immature and incredibly selfish of me to keep her. She wouldn't have been safe. It makes me so sad to think about you Gracie, but I did the right thing. After that I swore I would always be alone. It was and still is the closest I come to real crying.

My face screws up in pain and my eyes fill with anguish-laden salt water. But that's as close as I can get to actually crying emotionally. The tears never fall. Out of everything I've been through, that hurt the worst.

I didn't think anything could possibly hurt me anymore than I'd already been hurt, but I was wrong. After that, I gave up completely. I will never allow anyone close to me again.

People were always asking me if I had a boyfriend and why wasn't I married. I got sick of it, and I'd just say I'm gay. It actually helps to hide behind this sexuality; boys leave me alone - sometimes anyway. But I'm not gay, for the record. I am attracted to women and I loove big boobs, but it's hard for me with men, after everything (This gets so much worse after sewer rat). It takes time for me to trust. Also I haven't met anyone I like that way or that much yet. Nor am I even remotely capable of such a serious relationship?

My father is a prick, and he is weird, selfish and inappropriate. I met him when I was 17. He was always trying to kiss me on my lips. He is a selfish, nasty piece of poop. Every time I asked him for help or something, he'd say no, smiling evilly, spitefully and smugly, as if hurting me was some kind of victory to him.

When I was 18, I got a really Kool job and my boss was a fifty-year old guy. We actually got on well, one day, he asked me about my father.

Then he started acting all fatherly after I told him I never had one, and I was so far beyond stoked finally to have someone who wanted to be a father figure - too stoked to see the danger looming, to notice when he started touching my hips and making suggestive jokes.

One night, he suggested a scotch, which wasn't unusual. Then he raped me. It messed me up so bad. Even now, every time I think about it, I feel the hurt, disappointment, and confusion all over again. How could he do that to me? He took the only bit of trust I'd EVER formed and given away - he shattered my heart. WHY DOES EVERYONE WANT TO HURT ME ALWAYS? He is the first and last person I ever trust. I was so devastated. I got on a plane and moved to the other side of the country to stay with some family-in-law. I was hurting, so I behaved badly sometimes - not on purpose; I was drowning. I was so excited, thrilled and over the moon to finally have a father figure, but he only wanted to use me for sex. I got drunk one night and was forced again by a colleague.

However I felt a pull like no other and ended up back home and seeing my ex-boss because I was still so desperate for a father, but he just used me for sex and I couldn't stop it. I know it was weird and revolting, but I couldn't help it. I desperately needed a father figure, and I was trapped because of my childhood grooming. It was this weird combination of unfightable emotions with truly disturbing echoes from my past.

I was disappointed with myself but for six months, we had a mainly sexual relationship. I lived for the little moments

I felt like I had a protector and dad, just like when I was little, I lived for the moments when the men would pretend to be giants stomping their feet and then throw us girls around or tickle us or we listened to stories. At the end of the day, I'm just a little girl desperate for some semblance of family.

After we had sex, I would be so disgusted with myself; it was repulsive doing that with him. I'd cut long deep gashes in myself right after. I tried to kill myself and almost succeeded in an attempt to break the weird hold he had over me, but I could not escape. I drank, I drugged, but he turned up at the hospital, I couldn't leave.

Although he didn't force me after the first time, it was just as traumatic because I didn't want to do it. I was driven by an intense need to have a father that cared in my life and trapped in some strange, inexplicable sexual prison that held creepy, disturbing echoes from my childhood. In my defence: there is an in-built, intrinsic desire that drives children to strive for and do anything and to gain their parents approval and love. So this would have also contributed.

He knew what he was doing, taking advantage of a young girl lost, hurting and desperate for affection and attention, desperate for a father and protector. NB: this sort of relationship can be characterised as Stockholm syndrome, where you develop a psychological/emotional bond with captor/s or abuser/s; they use it to manipulate and control you. He kept me prisoner, refusing to let go.

I always had bosses and older male and female colleagues hitting on me before this, and I got fired a few times for refusing to go out on a date with the boss. For a while, I would go to clubs and pick up men, usually the bouncers, and I'd go back to their place and bahaha, ask the poor guys for a pair of boxers and a t-shirt to sleep in.

I did not have sex with them, just couldn't stand being alone when the nightmares were bad. I needed male company. I needed protection and to be near a big strong man. It was not sexual at all. I'm actually really lucky none of them hurt me.

In high school when my nightmares got bad, I would sometimes go to my best friend Mary's just to sleep. Neither of us understood it, but on some level, I guess she knew I couldn't stand to be alone and just was there for me. Mary has been a constant strength through my young adult life, such a kind and caring nature. Your awesome, girl.

There were a couple times when I had to pay a very high price for the affection I desperately needed and I let men use my body. I'm ashamed to admit it, but this vicious, unrelenting need overcame me and rational thought was not possible. I desperately needed male company and I would let them use my body to get it (only twice, and both ended up being my boyfriend).

But after my boss tricked me into trusting him, then hurt me, keeping me prisoner in a Stockholm syndrome type relationship — The abuser makes their victim become attached, addicted and kind of fall in love with and need them — I didn't want to be in, that was when I got my fire when it came to men and sex. I swore no man would ever hurt me again. I promised myself.

I hated men. After a bad jet skiing accident, I needed a bit of help for a few years. Mum was absolutely awesome; she gave up everything and worked so hard to get me back on my paws.

I had a few male helpers who hit on me. One even kissed me and got me to touch his dick. Which I did because I felt I had no choice even though I didn't want to. Yuk. There are certain situations in which I'm rendered completely powerless, especially if I'm vulnerable and someone is meant to be taking care of or protecting me. Because of the way I was groomed as a child, I always must submit, allow and cooperate when a man wants or does something sexual, even if I don't want to (or he'll beat me up and make me anyway)

Then I met a driver I called my spanky Possum, who was the first man I'd ever met who never showed any sexual interest in me. He had a huge positive impact on my life. We got on well and would laugh and have a great time. One day he said something to me that would change my life forever. I was a bit sad and he brushed my hair off my face and said, 'Don't worry, you're still lovable.' I felt like he'd just dropped a bomb on my world. Wait. WHAT?!Me? Loveable??? Since when?

This was the first time I'd ever been introduced to the notion of myself as loveable. It hadn't even occurred to me I was likeable! I knew men found me attractive, but likeable, loveable? Because the accident physically forced me to stop moving and running for a little while, I could no longer escape my past. I finally told my mum almost 20 years later that it wasn't just the teenage boy who hurt me. It was 9 different men then and countless boys and men over the years. Mum was beside herself with shock, anger, and despair. But it bought us closer.

I sought help at a place called Brave Hearts that specialises in child sex abuse. I saw two separate counsellors, who both fled the room in tears before I'd even gotten to the really bad stuff. It made me furious. Why the hell were they crying? You weren't the six- year-old who was held or tied down and raped, who was tortured, beaten and forced to watch as her friends were hurt. I thought what if it was a small child who was being brave talking to them and they behaved like that?

This is one of the biggest reasons why I've gone into counselling, because people who have been hurt need someone who is strong. I lived in hell for most of my life, and I came out stronger and more understanding. They needed me in this sector.

Anywayz, so Possum helped me track down a top specialist. He knew I'd been hurt and as we sat in the waiting room, I was shivering with anxiety. He put his arm around me and held me till she called me. She didn't cry, but I could still see it getting to her halfway through, and I couldn't stand it and ran from the room. I slid down the wall and onto the floor. Possum sat next to me as people stared at us judgingly.

We sat there for almost an hour till I finally found the strength to get up. Nothing about this was fair, other people getting upset over what happened to me. Possum was the male role model I needed, a true gentleman with a pure, kind heart and finally I saw how men should behave. We are still close friends. I am so grateful I finally have a man in my life who doesn't hit on me. We are completely at ease together and talk about anything and everything. He gave me an idea of what to look for in a man, if one ever catches my attention.

So far none have though … no spank you. I forced myself to date those few when I was younger, mainly because I knew I had to train myself to be able to put up with and then enjoy a man's touch. At first, I would yell at the poor boys. I even punched a few. But I eventually got to the point where I could stand it. Occasionally I could make myself come. Just to be clear here, not climax. There is a big difference, in case you didn't know. But I could rub my clit and could make my body come, and even if I didn't always feel pleasure, I enjoyed the closeness.

It was all just fun and games to me though, which I probably should have told the boys who eventually left with broken hearts. You see there's only one way I can deal with having people in my life: I need to be in control. Otherwise, if I get hurt by someone I'm fond of, it hits me hard and I can't deal. I am, as Hol says, oversensitive because of my lack of actual healthy human relationships. I'm not intimately close to or fond of many people, but this way, I'm in control. I only tell people little bits of information. Only scraps, never enough pieces to even see a fraction of my big picture.

I hide it all so well. This is where my intellect makes me slightly like an evil supervillain. I manipulate everyone close to me. Not in a big or bad way, just in the way they feel about me. Essentially, if people like me, it's because I let them; if people leave me, it's because I pushed them away and let them think it was their choice. It's the only way I can stand it. I can feel you judging me. I really do care and am not mean to people on purpose or anything. Actually, I'm the polar opposite; I care deeply for and lift people up, help them see how awesome, unique, and important they are.

But for so long, I had no control over how I was treated and what happened to me, so I had to find a way to cope. I'm so talented I even fooled Holly, who knows me so very well. For a while anyway, but eventually she started to notice my affection and 'I love yous' were fake.

I genuinely adore and care about Holly. But I say this exact line to many people. Sometimes if I'm very close to them, or if I know they would benefit from or need to hear those words, I will say, 'I love you,' although it's devoid of any actual feeling and emotion from me whatsoever. Love is such a powerful emotion, and I'm using it to heal the world. I heard of a study someone did once, I think Masaru Emoto, got four bottles of water he wrote the words love, kindness, hate and anger on them. After twenty-four hours, he examined the water under a microscope.

The bottles with love and kindness were filled with pretty colours and nice molecular patterns, and the ones with hate and anger had turned diseased and ugly. This is why I say I love you if someone needs to hear it. But it's all fake, even with Hol and Bunny. It's only a surface-level expression, nothing real.

Studies show kind words help plants grow, this works on humans and animals as well. Nevertheless I don't think I would or even could ever feel anything real.

Holly and I are soulmates. We are in love and we make love, but it's not romantic love. It's best friend, soulmate connection feelings. Honestly, the fact that I am capable of that much is amazing.

One day, Amy booked a massage for me with some random guy who turned out to be a sleazy, disgusting, perverted, predator. The first day, he was really nice and we were sort of friends, but I left the session filled with inner turmoil and fighting an intense desire to drink and hurt myself which I did not understand at the time. I was excited because his massage helped my injured limb after the accident and it was the first thing that really helped.

After a couple of massages, he changed into the despicable person he really was, once taking his dick out resting it on my head as he massaged my neck and shoulders! I know, hey. Messed up and absolutely appalling! But because of my ingrained childhood grooming, I was once again a victim. I couldn't do a thing about it — was terrified into stone.

But if he'd done it to one of my friends, or anyone else I knew, I would have gone over there with a baseball bat, mainly because a tiny cute blonde girl just really isn't particularly intimidating or scary and he sounded like a prick. I wouldn't have had any intention to hit him unless I had to protect myself, just to show that I was serious. Then I would have calmly spoken to him about his inappropriate behaviour and threatened to ruin his reputation and beat him with the bat if he ever did it again, but because it was me he did it to, I had no fight. I thought this was just how people treated me.

Before I move on, I just want to clarify here; I don't go around hitting people with baseball bats or hurting people. I fight only to protect myself and others. Usually I just use my words and carefully considered venomous threats, and this works well enough.

However, hypothetically having to walk into a stranger's place alone, to stick up for someone he had hurt and taken advantage of, and him sounding the asshole he is, I would have needed back up. Nevertheless, I'd never put anyone else in a dangerous situation like that. Hence the bat.

Then he started taking advantage of and using me. Once again, I didn't want to, but had no choice. He made me feel like if I didn't do what he wanted, he'd stop my massages -the one thing that was actually working-. Amy told him prior to my first massage that I had an extremely inappropriate sense of humour and that I'd been hurt and abused before, that monster knew I'd been abused before. I told him the same on the first day, explaining that my jokes are never a 'come-on' or invitation, and also that I was gay.

Still, he took advantage of and hurt me, bullied and manipulated me into sexual stuff and sucking his dick (puuke, he was so gross). Because he was my therapist, an older boy and a predator, I was instantly trapped. Yet again, my childhood grooming patterns took over and I was stuck, exploited and addicted, a prisoner in yet another horrible situation.

Then he turned inexplicably mean, even though when he was forced to take a week off sick, I gave him $400 of my own money to help cover his rent, etc: I was desperately trying to keep him on side so he wouldn't withhold the one thing helping me. This is called 'fawning' which is a trauma response, I.e. you do your best to please and fawn over your abuser so they won't get worse and hurt you more.

However, I often give money to people if they need it - as part of my reuniting the world, leading by example and pay it forward movements. Plus, I'm only in charge and control of my own behaviour and reactions.

Still, he was so cruel. He was delusional, he made up fake reasons to be really mean, nasty and horrible to me (a bit like mum). He started getting me to do sex stuff before he started; he would then refuse to do the massage and still made me pay him! That vile scum made me pay him to sexually, emotionally and psychologically abuse me!! Even when he occasionally actually did the massage he stopped doing it properly. He would brag to me about assaulting and taking advantage of other women sexually, too.

When I started trying to stick up for myself, he got much worse — typically manipulative narcissistic behaviour: he blamed me for my reaction to his disrespect — and then he called me toxic and abusive when I stuck up for myself and wouldn't let him bully, manipulate and take advantage of me anymore.

It was so awful, he was so nasty it totally broke my confidence and made everything worse. I put up with it for as long as I possibly could because the massage helped at first; then he stopped doing the one thing that worked, just used and abused me.

I stopped going back, and he started saying truly horrible, nasty things about me to my friends and other people and making up lies. He almost drove me to suicide.

I would leave each massage in extreme distress, feeling horrible and all torn up, even after I broke free, which was not easy, I almost committed suicide and for a long time after, I still quite seriously considered ending my life numerous times just to try to stop the pain of how bad he made me feel. Not only did he take advantage of me sexually, he took advantage of my kindness.

Then he pretty much destroyed all the work my friends had done building my confidence and convincing me I wasn't hideous and horrible, and he withheld the one thing helping me. It nearly broke me and I came so very close to jumping off a cliff. Like, for real, but a stranger grabbed my shirt and forcefully dragged me back to safety. (Spank you) We nicknamed him sewer rat (this is insulting to sewer rats). However, it was this, well, rather eyebrow-raising experience that led me to the men that would change things for me completely.

Dr Anthony Markus was a friend of someone I knew. Dr Anthony is an older man, very talented in natural health. The very first time I met him, I felt a strong connection and always felt completely at ease and ok to be myself, even when I was struggling. We became close as time passed and I got more accustomed to him. He is my dad, not biologically, but he is the man who was always meant to be my dad. I truly understood the concept of 'trusting God's plan' after meeting him.

My actual father was a pigheaded, selfish idiot and not good enough for me, but God had someone much better lined up for that job. This was not an easy thing for me to accept and I was filled with tumultuous turmoil, fighting a new kind of inner battle. However, Dr Anthony was very patient and understanding, reassuring, and kept proving himself gently. Eventually the storm within me grew quiet and calm and I let him in. He gets more of the real me then I usually show people.

He proves to me over and over he actually cares through his words, actions and kind, loving gestures, always going above and beyond.

One night, he dropped everything and left halfway through a special family dinner out at a restaurant, to come and help me with a shoulder brace that wasn't on correctly and causing me pain after I broke my shoulder badly. Every single time he proves he cares, or he hugs me, I heal just a little bit more. People frequently say to me that they feel so safe and secure in my arms and presence, like they are home.

I never really understood this sentiment until Dr Anthony hugged me in a loving, fatherly way. Holding me tight, trying to ease my emotional pain. I felt at home, I finally know what it feels like to have a caring father, something else I never thought I'd get to experience. He makes me grateful and happy. I feel such genuine happiness, almost elation. So as weird, convoluted and damaging as the massage rat experience was — it was so hard for me to let a strange man put his hands on my body, and yet again I was hurt, taken advantage of, and had my trust broken — it led me to my dad. So I can't regret it.

Because I still needed massages for circulation, I keep looking and by divine intervention, I find a man: the son of Zeus and he is what saved my life. He was my proverbial knight in shining armour. He treated me with respect and behaved with honour and integrity, I've never felt so safe with a man and this was right after the revolting massage rat. He was such a gentleman and we chatted and laughed. It is this man who changes everything for me emotionally.

I was thrown from one extreme to the other, from a sewer rat to a King. He didn't know the details or how bad it was, but he made me feel so safe, he helped me see I wasn't the problem. I was totally at ease. I'm usually not girly or feminine around men, which is a defence/protection mechanism. I make sure I'm the dominant personality in the room, but I knew I was safe with him. It didn't even bother me having his hands on my bare skin (normally I can't stand it; it makes me angry and terrified). I'd never before fantasized about being with a man, until I met him, but the idea of being in his arms, being close to and intimate with him, excited me, in a romantic and sexual way. This was a complete first for a male! Big surprise and another huge step forward.

It's this man who introduces me to the somewhat scary but exhilarating idea, that I might even be able to want to make love with and have a proper relationship with a man one day, which was something I never wanted or even dreamed was slightly possible. He had to move. After him I stop the massages because I just can't stand being alone with or touched by anyone else strange, male or female, even more so after the sewer rat guy.

You're going to think this next part is pathetic and sad and I would totally agree except that it's real. Such strong, genuine emotion that moves me in some deep, untainted place every time I think about it. It's kind of a prince charming and sleeping beauty story except I'm an emotionally dead kitten and prince charming is a little bit of a prick to be honest. One random day, I was walking through the shopping centre with a mate and this guy stops me. I ran my eyes slowly up his huge muscly body till I meet soul-piercing blue eyes. He was a huge fireman (from the calendar). Very sexy, even though I'm not usually attracted to men! No spank you. I'm not interested, but he is persistently asking if I have a boyfriend and checking my left hand for a ring.

I shoot Ally an annoyed glance and try to side-step him but can't and eventually I give him my number and escape.

Ally and I collapse with laughter as soon as we were far enough away. He invited me to have a drink with him, and I said no for obvious reasons. But a few days later he texted me to ask if I want a visitor. My girl had just cancelled our catch up on the Friday night, and I was like ok, yeah. I can have a fireman friend.

So he came over. I am accustomed to men turning up dressed nicely to take me to an expensive dinner date. This guy turned up in like old gym clothes, walked in the door and kissed me hard. Ummm, presumptuous much? We went into the living room and he commented on my nice place, then kissed me again, hands roaming. I was too affronted and confused to really react, luckily for him! So he fingered me a bit and then got his dick out and started trying to get me to bend over or suck it. Ahh, excuse me, Mr Sexy Fireman? What.The.Hell! We hadn't even had a drink; clearly he has women happy to put out on demand because he's so sexy. I had never been treated so disrespectfully by a man before.

He had a really nice dick, though. (Not that I have much experience in this department.) Then he kept asking, so I kicked him out. But the strangest thing happened; about an hour later, I realised I was aroused and that I enjoyed him touching me and kissing me. If I'm completely honest this is the very first time I've ever felt true, relaxed, easy sexual pleasure from/with another person, like ever. This was also the incredibly significant moment when my childhood grooming pattern was broken. I didn't feel I had to bend over or blow him. I was still really angry, hurt, revolted and reeling after the disgusting massage rat and I promised myself I'd never let it happen again. Plus, because of the strange and almost mystical effect the fireman had on me, I won. I broke it! HELL FREAKING YEAH, BABY.

Feeling arousal, pleasure, and enjoyment from a man's intimate touch was an interesting new experience. Not just that though; even though he was here for literally five mins if that, and behaved badly for most it, I enjoyed his company, and the little chatting we did was easy, fun and interesting. I was so confused and couldn't work out what was happening, but I knew I wanted to see him again. I noticed my face felt strange. I looked in the mirror. I was smiling, like for real. It was the strangest feeling.

I could not stop smiling. It took me a few days to get used to the feeling of smiling for real. I had to keep looking at my face in the mirror to see what it was doing, so confusing. It had been so long since I'd smiled properly, but I was disgusted and angry with myself afterward. I had gotten to this point without any real feelings and was happy to continue that way. The only way to protect myself from more hurt and bad people was to be alone. But this man walked his sexy butt into my life and changed everything for me sexually.

A couple of months later, I get triggered by a inappropriate hypnotherapist who was meant to be helping me with the abuse stuff but instead spent most of the time running his eyes over my hot bod and making me uncomfortable. One session, I was telling him a really traumatic memory of being molested, then raped when I looked over at him and he had this weird smile on his face. Kind of like the Grinch, so I was triggered into self-destruction and need for male company after that session with him, and I texted the fireman: come bang me.

He was at the gym but happily came right over. I met him at the door in nothing but kitten ears. I've never seen a man take his clothes off so fast; I thought he might fall over. To my astonishment, I completely enjoyed banging him and him using his tongue. There was no undercurrent of anger, revulsion, guilt, fear or confusion like there normally was. Amazingly, there was just genuine arousal, excitement and pleasure.

It was awesome, exciting, confusing. It took a while for me to stop hating myself after that. The next morning, I started drinking just after 7 am. But eventually I stopped being angry at myself and I was so very excited. I didn't even feel I had to hurt myself! If one man could make me feel like this, maybe there were more. Maybe there was one for me. I told Holly, who tried to be happy for me, but I could see her sadness and knew that must have hurt her after being by my side for so many years and fighting so hard.

Constantly jumping into the darkness to save me every time I fell in. After all that, it was someone else who held the key. And a male, just to rub salt in.

We banged once more a month later, but I couldn't take it. He messed me up to the point I couldn't think straight. I had so many new feelings I had to explore, understand and accept. A few months later, I invited him over to talk to him about his place in my life and subsequently, this novel. He came over in a bad mood and was not at all the sweet, kind gentleman I had glimpsed through his bad behaviour. I knew he was behaving that way because he was hurting. Not just PTSD, but a woman had hurt him. I also knew that my loving, caring nature could set him free (as friends)

But he was too pigheaded, proud, a bit silly and caught up in his pain. Having studied human behaviour from a distance all my life, I am an expert at reading people and can quickly and accurately discern and evaluate their psychological problems.

So he came over in a bad mood, and I couldn't see my sweet, kind fireman at all. He was cold and distant and annoyed. I tried to explain to him the impact he had, but he was gone. The sweet man who tried to get me to open up and trust him had disappeared. It doesn't matter, because he had already played his extremely important part in my life and set me free - filled me with hope and happiness.

These two men are the reason I finally sat down to finish writing this; I have been writing bits of it in my head since

I was small. But it was them and the feelings they awoke in me that changed everything. Sweet boys, you were my princes. You were the key and you set me free. Spank you.

This is only the most important part of the fireman story; mostly he didn't treat me very well, but he did say some nice things to me. He made me feel special. Even though he doesn't seem to deserve the accolades, I promise you he does. He has a fractured personality from his PTSD and past relationships, but he made me feel safe and feel pleasure without knowing my background or changing his behaviour to be more gentle or patient, and that screams so much louder than his bad behaviour.

We had quite a few sweet moments, looking into each other's eyes and grinning like fools for ages and he tried to get me to open up and lower my weapons once. I'm not mistaken. He is a good man under all that pain, and I am grateful I met him.

They made me want so many things. I'd never wanted to share my life with anyone until I met the son of Zeus, never enjoyed kissing or being touched by a man intimately until the fireman. Never given a proper relationship any serious consideration and never, ever imagined sex could feel that good. They are a big part of my happy ending, and I am truly grateful to them for their place in my life.

I wish the fireman would have let me help him, but we have not been in contact since he came over so different. (There's no way I'm putting up with that behaviour)

For reasons I'll never understand, some people have always treated me badly, like, been mean to/ bullied me. When I was young, it really hurt my feelings.

But when I was a teenager, I started to suspect it was jealousy, at least from some people. I have always been loud, fun, funny and wild, a potent combination in a smart, cute, sexy, naughty girl. Holly confirmed this years later. She said to me one day, 'Geez, Kit. Some people are such dicks to you sometimes, hey?' I nodded mutely.

She wrapped her arms around me pulling me into a hug, and said, you know why, don't you?' I nodded. 'Yep. Because I'm a piece of worthless shit.' 'No, baby. Because they are jealous. You are a giant with your big, brave, kind, loving heart and unique sex appeal, power and magic. They feel small, insufficient, insecure and insignificant standing next to you.' This made me feel slightly better. Maybe it wasn't because of something I was doing wrong.

Sometimes I'm not sure I can trust Holly's opinion of me; she seems to see something I can't. Ok, I will concede, still somewhat reluctantly, that yes, thanks to her, now I know I'm ridiculously wicked fun, Kick Ass Kool, have a great personality and a huge kind heart. Because of her, I see that now.

A very large part of me still feels like I'm not enough and never will be worthy of anything. But I recognise that's wrong, even if I can't change the feeling.

Hol and I spend many hours examining and dissecting the strange, ridiculous behaviour that my mere presence seems to evoke in others sometimes. It's quite amusing at times -she thinks it is jealousy or coz they are in love with me.

Psychology is her passion also and together we delve into complex human nature and unravel the intricate interconnected webs of emotions and behaviours. This is mainly why I make such a great counsellor, but partly because I understand, thanks to Holly, the power of love. I harness it and use it to help my clients and I am very successful.

After studying everyone, which is something I still do today, I also realised some people are just mean and it had nothing to do with me. Someone was hurting them first. Bullies generally bully because they are hurting or being bullied too, and no one is helping them. It's a cry for help in a twisted way.

The pain gets so unbearable and I can't stand it. I reach out, but no one and nothing can lessen it. I sometimes wake in the morning after horrible nightmares of being abused and have to deal with my body. I hate it and I don't think of being hurt, but I just need to come, so I do think of random things like the laundry I need to do. Then I hate myself. I know now from my research many adults who were abused as children experience this. I remind myself of this often.

Nothing has been easy for me. Watching everyone with their loving, caring families and mums and dads always made me so sad. Just seeing the other kids happy, loved and with plenty of food was a constant reminder that for some reason I wasn't worthy or enough to be loved, cared about or fed properly. I'd stand in front of the mirror, looking at myself hard; trying to find/see what was so horrible about me.

It frustrated me and made me sad and angry because I only saw a broken-hearted little girl looking back, just a regular kid. Now I'm almost grown, it's just as hard watching my friends with their loving husbands, kids, and families, something I know I won't ever get to experience. I'm quietly really, really sad about missing out on that, but you can't tell because I'm smiley and cheeky and funny and inappropriate, always so talented at hiding my pain.

But, after meeting the son of Zeus, my secret is that I'd love a big strong man to come up, wrap his arms around me protectively, hold me tight, and say, 'I'm here baby, I got you.' I would secretly like to experience a loving romantic and sexual relationship with a good man.

I feel so envious watching my friends so happy with their husbands and children and knowing this has been stolen from me, like my childhood, like my innocence, my happiness, my life. I am slowly learning to accept myself.

Over the years, I've spoken to and counselled many other abused people and researched psychological and physical effects and found that most of what I feel and have experienced is not unique to me. As I'm writing this, I know there are other women and men out there confused hurting and lost, hating themselves, considering suicide, drinking, drugging, trying to escape the pain and darkness and I know it will help to know you aren't alone and there are many things beyond your control and even comprehension. But, IT IS NOT YOUR FAULT. Never was and never will be.

There is never a circumstance in which the child is at fault. Children are innocent and too young and confused to understand what's happening. You cannot spend your life berating yourself, which is something I did for far too long. You cannot expect any child to be able to comprehend and deal with adult situations like this.

When I was a teenager, I used to go into the bush and I'd scream so loud and so long till my voice broke, then till I was hoarse, then till the only sound I could make was a faint rasp. I screamed for all the times I wasn't allowed to scream or cry when those men were hurting me, for all the times I was so frustrated with not being able to please my mum or anyone else. Nothing I did was ever good enough. I felt like I was living in a world where everyone spoke a different language to me and I guess in a way, that's the perfect analogy for the way my unique intellect, maturity and life experiences distinguish me from everyone else.

When I was in high school, I started to really notice the difference in my friends' families. There was love and laughter and unity, and no one else's dads seemed to hurt them. I realised how different I was because of my childhood.

I still had friends and fun in the end, but I secretly knew I was the alien (Angel) among them. When I first got my license, I would drive out into the country and scream until I couldn't make a sound.

Then I sit there and stare and listen to sad music, trying to puzzle out the mystery of life and why God thought it was fair to do this to me. I would sit and hurt so bad I thought I might explode. This is where I went when I disappeared on Holly. Sometimes I'd drink myself to the point I could not stand. Obviously didn't drive then. Slept in my 4wd. I tried to make myself cry and feel, but I couldn't. To be honest, I don't want to. I'm sick of being hurt, and the only way to protect myself is to not feel and be alone.

One night, Hol calls me late-ish and says, 'get dressed. We are going out. I'll be there in ten minutes.' I have no idea where we are going or how to dress, so I put on the dress I was wearing earlier. She picks me up and drives silently. I begin to get suspicious; she hasn't even kissed me hello. I rack my brain and have no idea where we are going or why. Hol pulls into a police station. It's not a station I go to often, so it can't be one of the boys' birthdays or anything.

She grips my hand a little too tightly as we go inside. After we walk past the front desk, like VIPs, like we are expected, the first thing I see is Amy, my tiny little bunny. She looks like she's fallen down some stairs.

She's in a hospital gown, and there are three boy cops standing to the side. I'm trying to work out why we are in a police station and not a hospital if Amy's fallen and hurt herself. I run my eyes over her and freeze mid step as I see the blood between her legs. She is barely wearing the gown, and you can see all her bits. I look back at her face, and realisation dawns on me slowly, hand in hand with despair, anger, sadness and anguish. She's been raped and beaten.

My heart starts to flutter. I can't focus; I know I'm slipping away, being pulled back through time, but I also know Amy needs me. It's a desperate internal struggle for me, I have to fight it. Then I realise the three male cops are standing there staring at Amy, whose legs are wide open as she slumps on herself, crying. It's enough to pull me back as rage surges through my veins, hot and raw. Amy looks like she's about nine in the oversized gown. She is still just a teenager, and the three adult policemen are standing there, openly staring at her like that.

I lose my head big time. I'm screaming at them but not even focusing on what I'm saying. I could have been yelling about bananas not belonging in fruit salad for all I knew. I am fighting an inner battle of emotions from my past and feeling like I'd failed Amy, who was my little sister in so many ways. I should have protected her, been around more. All of a sudden, my face feels funny; it's hard to breathe, and I feel all choked up. Then Holly is there, her arms around me. My face is wet. I must be sweating, but I realise Amy needs me, so I snap out of it and go to her.

The guys can't find any blankets or spare clothes. I'm seething in anger on Amy's behalf. 'Take off your shirt,'

I demand, but all three refuse. For a fleeting second I consider, in my boiling anger, tearing one of their shirts off, but I realise that would only result in me being arrested and possibly charged with assault, which was not what Amy needed right now, so instead I take my dress off and help her into it, leaving in nothing but Playboy lingerie. She calls me Sexy Back, insists that's my song, so I start singing it to her, but I feel all choked up again. It's hard to sing.

I don't know what's wrong with me. Later, Holly tells me I was crying. Not actual emotional crying, but I think all the anger, frustration and rage overflowed and leaked from my eyes. I do this sometimes under extreme duress, or if I'm very sick, but I maintain it does not count as normal emotional crying. I literally can't do that. There are no feelings attached to it, it's more like my eyes watering badly...

I carry Amy to the car, then go back and tear the guys to absolute shreds. In nothing but see-through lace lingerie, oh, that would have been a funny thing to watch. I'm a nice person, but if I need to, I can be angry and mean. You'd better run. Run fast and far. I speak to the senior police chief then the police commissioner. I promise you, after tonight and the epic tantrum I throw with threats of going to the international media; every police station on the entire continent now has a spare set of clothes and blankets. Then we take Amy home, give her some food, which she eats tenderly and slowly, and I work with her immediately. It's so hard to be tough right after an incident, especially with someone I care about, but it's so very important. Amy cries, but after a few weeks, I know she will be fine, no PTSD or anything.

I thought I should tell you some normal stuff about our lives. As you know, I am a very successful, exceptionally talented counsellor, and I have been told numerous times my help has saved and changed lives. I just literally do whatever is needed. I help with finances, relationships, I've taught men how to pick up women and vice versa, I've worked with families, I've gone out drinking with clients, and I've gone with them while they faced and confronted abusers or parents. I've gone to workplaces/schools to address bullying.

I'm a very affectionate counsellor (appropriately) I hug them when they cry, hold them or their hand if needed. I believe this is the very essence of being human; you just step up and do whatever is needed (within reason and boundaries) to help someone else. I do this for my friends too, strangers, enemies. I am immensely proud of this.

I'm also fit, sporty and love music. I'm a truly terrible singer. I do my absolute best to do my part for the world. I smile and compliment everyone who comes close enough saying, 'hey gorgeous, nice dress,' or, 'you look beautiful in that colour,' or just 'looking good, babe,' or something else encouraging.

Everyone smiles brightly, but occasionally I'll say something to someone who desperately needed to hear it and it's so rewarding watching their frown fade instantly and a huge beaming smile appear on their face.

At home, I use as little power as possible; the only things that stay permanently plugged in are the fridge, dishwasher and oven, and only because I can't reach the dishwasher and oven sockets. Everything else I plug in for immediate use, and then straight away unplug once finished! I turn the bathroom sink tap on to get hot water through, then turn it on in the shower only long enough to get wet, then off while I soap up, then on again for a quick rinse.

I recycle, don't allow food or water to go to waste where possible, and I only buy organic, I always support small businesses and pay in cash only. KEEPING CASH IS THE ONLY WAY TO KEEP OUR FREEDOM of speech, choice, movement, personal decisions…EVERYTHING. We give up cash; we lose control over our lives and choices. Also, I pick up litter and try to educate everyone where I can.

I do kind things and lend/ give money without expecting anything in return. If someone wants to repay me, I tell them to pass it on instead, pay it forward.

I 'm not really scared of much, except for random things touching me when I'm in the water. Even the pool or a bath! I have serious issues with it; it's my kryptonite. It makes me squirm just thinking about it. Uughh. Squeamish. My loofah brushed my arm in the shower once and I screamed so loud and numerous times until I realised what had touched me and why, my neighbours thought I was being assaulted and called the police when I didn't answer the door.

You should have seen the looks on their faces when I explained why I was screaming. They just went, 'You're kidding me.' I grinned, standing at my door in nothing but a towel, suggesting it would be a funny story to tell at the station, 'Called out to assist young girl attacked by loofah in shower.' I thought it was completely hilarious. They did not. I have had new neighbours call the police other times because of women screaming, repeatedly. I so very much enjoyed explaining that one.

'Sorry, officers. They were screaming and moaning in *pleasure*.' I even offered once, with my trademark cheeky grin, to prove it to the two young male police officers who came to investigate a call of women screaming and moaning loudly: 'come and watch if you don't believe me boys.' Yep. I'm that good. Apparently, the girls could be heard half-way down the street. I think this is one of the main reasons I'm still alive. God enjoys watching all the random shenanigans I get myself into.

Amy's parents are selfish jackasses who barely tolerate their two children, Amy and Jackson. They grew up with nannies that eventually left. It was a constant thoroughfare of carers for them. Amy had problems with self-destructive behaviours like alcohol, drugs, bulimia and being slutty because it gets her attention. All of this is understandable, given her childhood. She'd never had a proper Christmas or birthday when I met her.

The only time I glimpsed Amy's parents: We are at her parents' place in Paradise Point and Amy gets a phone call. Her voice is quiet as she talks, which makes me instantly curious. She gets off the phone, starts racing around, tidying up.

'Mum and Dad are here,' she whispers excitedly. 'They are actually coming home. I haven't seen them for three years.' We run around cleaning up. I hear a car pull in and retreat upstairs, but I'm watching from the landing. Her mother struts in with an air of importance.

Amy is standing right beside the door as her parents walk in. Her mother grunts at her in distaste, then walks in, not even acknowledging her daughter. I see Amy's shoulders slump and her head hang a bit. Her dad walks past her too, without even a sideward glance. He takes a few steps into the foyer and turns around. Amy cries, 'Daddy, I missed you.' And he smiles softly. 'Oh, pumpkin,' he says, opening his arms wide, and she practically flings herself into his arms in a move that's actually more like a football crash tackle. He has barely held her for a second when her mother barks, 'Oh, get off him, you little skank.'

Amy scampers away, defeated. My first instinct is to go down and yell at them, but I know Bunny is going to be humiliated if she knows I'd seen that and to be honest, they wouldn't care anyway, they clearly lacked the mental and emotional depth. They grab some stuff and leave immediately. I watch their Mercedes disappear, fury running through me.

I quietly tiptoe downstairs. I can hear her sobbing in the laundry; it makes me so angry and so sad. Unsure how to handle this, I give her five minutes, then softly tap on the door. She barely manages to get the words 'F off' out between her sobs. I don't, of course. I go into the bathroom part. I can smell vomit, which is her main way of self-harm: bulimia. We had largely got past that, though now I truly understood the origins of that disorder. She was embarrassed once she realised I'd seen it all. I smatter her head and little face with kisses and tell her she's beautiful and lovely.

She sits there on the floor, so small, sobbing her little broken heart out. It's freezing, so I pick her up and carry her to the downstairs bedroom. I wrap her in a blanket and pull her into my arms. She sobs sadly. 'Why?! Whhhyyyy do they hate me, Bella?'

'Oh, darling, it's not you they hate, it's themselves. Your mum is jealous because your dad loves you more than he loves her. She can't deal. Clearly no one ever loved her and she can't bear to share your dad and that isn't your fault, even though it's unfair. It's normal human nature.' I explained the cycle of abuse. 'This isn't your fault, sweetheart, you are perfect.

They have trouble loving themselves, which makes it hard to love anyone else, plus your mum's a bit of a stuck-up bitch.'

I explained it until she understood and realised it was not her, but them. She stopped crying and promptly fell asleep in my arms. I kissed her sweet little face; she makes this odd sound when she sleeps when she's exhausted, kind of like a little bunny mewing. This is how she got her nickname.

I can't believe how her parents treated her, and I'm still furious with myself and deeply regret not saying something, not sticking up for her, not working with them until they saw sense, until they saw their beautiful daughter so desperate for their love and attention. She mirrored my own anguish there, I wanted to make her feel happy, loved and appreciated, so I texted Hol about setting up a surprise party for Amy. No reason; just because, she'd never even had a birthday party, so we all brought presents. I made sure they were colourfully wrapped. I got fairy bread and kids' party food, and we played pass the parcel and had a three-legged race, which was so much fun we decided to repeat it often at our adult parties with alcohol involved (awesome fun, but a tad dangerous!).

Amy has all the joy and wonder of a little girl on her face, and I realise I need to be her parent, her mum, which was ok back when we had a platonic relationship. Over the years, I went from friend to mother to sister to bestie to lover, teacher and all over at different times. I just decided to be whoever she needed as situations arose. It sounds weird I know, but I believe this is the very foundation of being a good person: you step up, and you be and do whatever someone needs you to, again, within reason. But Amy needed me to be her everything, so I was.

It is a weird relationship for sure, but I saved her from drugs, drink and self-harm. I'm never going to have children. Even if I had another miracle conception, I couldn't carry it to term after the knives, tools, and toothbrush case. So those first few years with Amy, I gave her the best Christmas and birthdays and was the mum she never had. Also the mum I'd never get the chance to be. I would have been a great mum too.

I have not seen her parents again, and I wish I could go back to that day and confront them, barricade them inside, and work with the family. Make them look at Amy; make them see the sweet little fairy she is.

In the beginning, Amy would go on drinking benders. She'd let strangers, not just men, use her body. She would drink and do drugs, throw up whatever she ate. The first time, I didn't realise till she came back what she was doing; the second time, though, I had a plan. I watched for the signs, and after a couple weeks, I went after her. I rented a room near Byron, and I Amynapped her. I had to actually tie her to the bed to get her through the worst of the detox, and not in the sexy way I usually tie girls up.

I hated watching her suffer. I used wet flannels to cool her down. I bought healthy, nutritious food and practically force fed her, but as she got better, I made it fun. I bought snorkelling gear, and I distracted her with naked snorkelling and beach adventures. I rented movies and got yummy snacks. I gave her facials.

We made up our own body scrub, and after exfoliating each other naked, much to the delight of a few groups of random strangers who had wandered onto our private beach, we had spa baths and used our homemade body moisturiser and scrub.

I bought her some pretty dresses, and we went out to dinner. I did my best to be her family and her best friend, and she came good. I reminded her how nasty those first ten days were if I thought I was losing her, and I also emphasised I'd do anything for her and chase her down every time. I promised I'd come find her every single time she got lost. In spite of all that, she's lovely, kind and thoughtful. She's tiny and small with a porcelain doll face.

She's timid and extremely naive; she wouldn't say 'boo' to a goose, mainly because if a goose, even a baby one, came within three feet of her, she'd run away screaming, so she couldn't even get close enough to say 'boo' to it anyway. But when it comes to it, she digs deep and finds courage I didn't realise she had. She once crash tackled our ex-friend Shelly, who was an almost six-foot-tall supermodel (who reminded me a bit of Cruella de'Vil from 101 Dalmatians) into the pool after she was nasty to me.

Another time in da club, she stepped up behind me while I was taking on two huge Russian bullies and squeaks that I have backup. The entire club was watching and roared with laughter, including the two huge men. But I have never been prouder of her.

She must have been terrified inside, but still she stepped up for me. Just for the record, I could handle the boys alone just fine. But it's the thought that counts.

I've spoken of my soulmate connection with Holly, who I'll get to next, but Amy and I have an intense connection too. Part of it is trauma bonding, but most of it is an inexplicable attraction to and understanding of each other.

When our eyes met the first time, we both felt it instantly, and it only strengthened as our friendship grew its lightning and thunder, swirling with magic, and there were times we would lie together on the beach or wherever just looking into each other's eyes, talking but not saying a word. The fierce connection intangible, but simultaneously a thick, indestructible concrete bridge between us. When she giggles, it's literally like a sweet song, like wind chimes in the wind. You can't help but like her.

One day, we are walking down the esplanade at Surfers looking for somewhere to swim. She stops me and says, in total innocent sincerity: 'babe, I've got a bun in the oven.' She was my girlfriend at the time, and I thought this was a really rude shock and strange way to tell me she'd cheated on me. 'I need to deal with it right now.' She looks desperate. I explain, 'you have to book an appointment and go to the doctor.' It turns out she was trying to tell me she had to poop badly. What a relief.

Holly, on the other hand, is very much like me. Headstrong, confident, resilient and smart. You don't get away with anything with Holly. Treat her right or bugger off. She's not afraid to speak up or stand up and fight. I am exactly the same; together, we are a very strong, sexy, elegant, formidable team.

Hol and I have a very similar amount of crazy. We once got smashed at a Sydney casino and ran a serious muck (amok). It was so much fun; we blew through over 10k in less than a week, some of it just tipping concierge boys stupidly large amounts of money to tell us if our boots matched our jeans or asking if they liked our tits and other truly ridiculous stuff.

We went snowboarding too. We love to tease boys, make out in clubs just to score free drinks and tease all the boys. We go on long, random road trips. I know she wants me to love her back and be her life partner, but I can't. I truly want and need to be alone. It's the only way I feel safe. It's my homeostasis. We will always be best friends, though.

Jasper, who you briefly met, is like my younger brother. I kind of raised him. He is such a great man and a true gentleman. He is the only boy who's a friend that I've really been close to other than my bestie, Moodle.

People always think I'm a slut or easy because I'm flirty, cheeky and affectionate, but I'm actually not at all. Ok, yeah, occasionally when I'm drunk and there's a hot girl with big tits, or, umm (said with slightly amused shame) ... a stripper. I can misbehave, but I've been with 12 people my whole life. Occasionally, I'd let guys feel me up a bit if I was desperate for male company, but it's been a very long time since I did any of that. It's something I find frustrating because people think less of you and treat you like you're less if they think you're slutty.

It's stupid. Everyone is so judgemental! I just accept and love everyone. We all have our own and are moulded/built by our unique stories and experiences.

Just putting it here, for the record, for the haters out there:

I'M NOT EASY, OR SLUTTY. 😎

I have a cool plan. I'm going to write this novel; then I'm going to help with conservation efforts, etc. then I'm going to use the money from that to buy huge amounts of land. I'm going to make it paradise: I'm going to adopt all the homeless and abused animals (from labs, slaughter houses etc.) the children no one wants and bring them to live with me. Then I'll get all the homeless and old people with no family and anyone else who wants to come, and then everyone will have a family and be loved. We can all take care of each other, one big family where no one is left out. This will be my legacy; a utopian community. We will grow our own organic food and share it. Animals will roam happily and freely in healthy sun filled pastures. Only eaten when they die naturally.

In school, kids will be taught about companion planting (natural pest control), organic farming, water purification and building shelters. Also how to communicate properly and help others, as well as standing up for what's right and other important and appropriate behaviours and life skills. We will all help and love each other and everyone will have all they need. There will be no war or threats of a scary freedomless, nightmarish future. No tyranny. Everyone will be safe.

I think at this point after reading this far, some of you might think I'm crazy or strange with the weird sex stuff! It's literally textbook side effects from child abuse, and as for the rest of it, before you make up your mind about me being crazy; let me tell you a story:

Amy, Zoe, Hol and I jump into the car to do a bottle-o run at Amy's dinner (however we generally don't actually eat dinner; it's more like an alcohol-filled all girl sex party). I have been drinking since Zoe picked me up at four. She is the designated driver. We are singing the spice girls, of all things, at the top of our lungs; I'm half hanging out the window.

All of a sudden, there are flashing lights behind us. We pull over and a female and two male cops get out. Holly says, 'Three police; they must know you're here, Kitten.'

The girl is cute. I'm still half hanging out the window as she walks up. 'Hey, gorgeous,' I, well, kinda slur to be honest and shoot her a cheeky smile. Someone kicks me. She smiles at me. One of the boys clears his throat. 'Hi, boys,' I say, giving them a little wave, and then turn my attention back to her.

She is enjoying my attention and smiling at me as I tell her she looks smoking hot in that uniform. I tell her I have my own police uniform and ask her if she would like to see it; I tell her we could play policewomen, that I will arrest her for once. The boys love it. I tell her I've been a bad girl; she giggles and says she can see that.

Amy, whose kicks I have been ignoring, forcefully pulls me back into the car and starts kissing me, which I later learn was an effort to get me to shut up. It worked extremely well. She gives Zo a breath test, and when I finally break free, I turn my head to see the boys watching us with tents in their pants. Very professional boys I giggle.

I ask the girl for a kiss goodbye, but she says she can't because she's on duty, which I'm claiming is not technically a no. I'm claiming that. Not a no, an 'I can't'.

They let us go. Amy slaps me across the arm a little too hard and tells me I almost got us arrested and am now banned from bottle-o runs. To my surprise, she actually enforces this and next time I have to stay home, so I drunk text people I shouldn't, like the fireman and a few random people.

They are gone for ages, so I go into Amy's room and rearrange everything, hiding things in weird places. I put most of her underwear in the kitchen, some in the letterbox and then I go around to her neighbours' houses and introduce myself as Amy's secret sex slave. I am now unbanned from bottle-o runs. I am banned from being left alone for too long. Hehe.

Anywayz, so am I crazy?

HELLS YEA BABY!

BUT IT'S FUN.

One night, I'm at home and I hear one of my neighbours being beaten up by her husband, a very large scary man who doesn't like me because every time I hear him getting angry and throwing stuff I go knock on the door with a smirk and ask if everything's ok. I can hear him beating her really hard, so I get dressed and get on to 000. I explain and they say they are backed up and won't be able to send help for at least an hour.

'She'll be dead by then,' I counter. All she says is, 'Sorry, best we can do.' So I ask her to please send three ambulances in the meantime. She asks why three and I explain the wife is going to need one for sure.

I have no idea what condition the two small kids are in, and she says, 'and the third one?' I reply that I'm not going to stand by and let him beat her to death, that I'm going in with my baseball bat to try to defend/help/ save her.

The woman on the phone argues with me, and I reply, 'Well, even if you guys came right now, lights and sirens, I'd still go in, so please organise the three ambulances and try to hurry. It's going to either be me or him leaving in the third ambulance.'

I grab my bat and go and knock on the door; he opens it covered in her blood and furious at the interruption. He is standing to the right side of the door frame. I act fast, boot him hard as I can in the nuts and dart in behind him on his left and hit him in the soft spot in the back of his knees. He falls forward like a sack of potatoes. I don't want to hit him in the head with the bat unless it's a last resort because I could easily cause serious brain damage and/or death. The second he hits the ground I slam the door shut and lock it.

We are safely locked inside. I call the police and tell them only one ambulance is needed for her; the kids and I were fine.

I yell through the door that police were on their way, so assumed he was long gone. With no keys or phone, he wouldn't go far though. The ambulance came and without problem took her to hospital. When the police finally show up almost two hours later, I'm standing in the hallway waiting. I make them show me their badges and then tell them, smiling, 'Well you're too late. I already did your job for you over an hour and a half ago, and the ambulance has come and gone. You have to go to the hospital.'

She has a couple of scars but is otherwise fine. She gets her sister to look after the kids, and the police want to give me a hero's commendation (again), which I gratefully and politely decline. I actually regret that. Maybe they could have given me a little certificate or something, but I try to remain anonymous where possible.

When I was a little girl, I was always alone. If I wasn't alone, I was being yelled at by my mum (my only family), who made sure I knew I wasn't loved liked or wanted, belittled me and made fun of me, with her friends, to my face. Or I was being beaten, tortured, raped, and worse by the nine men in a paedophile ring across the road.

You can't imagine how badly I hurt sometimes. A small child to be rejected by their own mother for a start shattered my little heart. I remember standing on the curb between the two houses, looking back at my home and knowing if I went there, my mummy would yell at me, often for things I hadn't even done. Or the other choice was to go to my friend's house and possibly be beaten, tortured and raped by nine disgusting men and a teenage boy.

I often chose the latter option because at least I felt wanted and accepted, in a strange way I got attention. Even though it was mostly bad, at least I felt part of something and wasn't alone.

When I was very small, before those men beat crying out of me, I used to wander off alone, find a place to sit in a tiny ball, and cry my little eyes out wondering why I was so horrible and no one liked me. I would cry so hard I couldn't breathe properly, sobbing so hard my entire body was shaking.

Even though I obviously didn't succeed in any of my 4 suicide attempts, I had still killed the essence of myself and was dead inside.

Holly helped me realise that different isn't necessarily bad. I'm different because I'm braver, stronger and more accepting, loving, kind and understanding than most people. When she said that to me, I truly saw myself, finally, just for a split second, as she saw me, as a giant and a superhero.

Suddenly I felt something I'd never felt before: pride. Maybe I wasn't as bad as I thought.

I realised after my fourth try that suicide clearly wasn't my destiny and God was probably still busy trying to kitten-proof Heaven, which I imagine includes covering all sharp edges and sound proofing walls, installing numerous stripper poles and bungy-jumping cranes, that sort of thing! Plus, you know, some sort of huge pot where I could melt large amounts of chocolate ... and, of course, upgrading his noise-cancelling headphones ... hehe.

So I became even more determined to heal myself, have fun, and keep trying to reunite and change the world and help, heal and inspire others.

After almost ten years of having Holly and Bunny in my life, building me up and chasing me into the darkness, things start to change. Slowly, the nightmares and trances become less frequent and intense. Instead of running out into the night in a trance, I go to the living room. Holly tirelessly chips away at the prison I built around myself and slowly my heart starts to thaw, for her at least. Everyone else I keep at arm's length in my little chess game.

It wasn't until I met the son of Zeus and the fireman touched me really, that I realised I could actually feel pleasure, enjoy sex and actually be attracted to men. Or, lol, man rather. So far, that's still singular. But I'm working on it; you don't go through what I have been through and come out the other side unscathed. I'm better at sex stuff now. For a long time, I couldn't stand to be touched by or even left alone with anyone strange, male or female. I still can't deal with anger, especially from men. Getting angry or upset with me, to my face, will result in me instantly shutting you out of my life. I can't deal. I barely give first chances; absolutely no second chances.

When I was a child, I was confused, hurt and scared. As an adult, I suffer greatly. The pain I feel is so intense, so deep and insurmountable. I am constantly looking over my shoulder and scanning faces in the crowd. I have never felt safe. I have never been safe. I still have occasional nightmares, but thanks to Holly's unwavering, loving dedication, I no longer run out into the night in a trance, desperately trying to escape the pain and horror.

Holly made me promise I would never leave her side, which I did solemnly, but I couldn't promise any tomorrows to anyone, not even myself. The girl I am is a result of my friends' love and loyalty, and my own fighting and breaking through the pain. They helped me a lot, but at the end of the day, it was me who battled the worst of the darkness. Sometimes it's so hard to hold on and rise above it all. No one really realises or gives me enough credit for how hard it is being strong and making it through each day and night.

Now I'm a successful, strong-willed young adult and one of the most remarkable people you could ever meet. Just walking around fighting to change the world, trying to reunite us all as a community once again! There's safety in numbers. Please join me in a #RETURNTOLOVE. One for all, all for one.

I get my happy ending. I got to feel attraction for a man and sexual pleasure with one. I start to recognise my worth and accept myself and slowly grow to like, then eventually love myself and, after the son of Zeus, Dr Anthony and the fireman, I feel real genuine happiness and joy. I got closer to Mum and she loves me now. I got to finally have a loving dad and even an awesome big brother.

I've made some real friendships and met people who helped me carry the heavy burden on my little shoulders.

Along the way, I had to learn how to stand up to bullies. I got tired of people pushing me aside like I don't matter. Now I am lethal. I will try kindness first because I understand people hurt others because they are hurting or being hurt themselves; if that doesn't work though, then I go for the jugular, with words, and I hit them hard enough they'll never do it again. I can, if pushed to it, reduce people to snotty messes rocking in a corner. But bullies will most likely never bully again after I do that. Learning to stand up for myself started with realising I don't deserve to be treated badly, and that was a hard but huge positive acknowledgment, then change.

I've never known how to feel about myself. Ok, I'm a good person right through, but I never really knew how to like me, so I just joined in with everyone else not liking me and treating me like crap. People took advantage of me and seemed to think they could walk over me coz I'm little and cute and cheeky.

People pushed me aside like I don't matter; I've never understood why. But I'm strong now. I can stand up for myself as well as everyone else.

I am doing what I set out to do: changing and reuniting the world by spreading love, light, kindness and leading by example. I have and will continue to change and improve people's lives by building them up and making them feel awesome, perfect and strong. I have impacted the world with this novel and my honesty.

I have saved many lives with my counselling and my kindness and generosity in general. I'm still doing random, crazy fun stuff too. So, if you see a hot brunette, drunk and naked, doing something stupid on the news ..... It's not me, I SWEAR. Hehe.

I was finally able to see myself as Holly and everyone else sees me. I finally see me as I actually am: strong, brave, funny, interesting, kind, loving, caring, fun, crazy, intense, worthy, enough, loveable, loved, liked, wanted, important and now I'm happy and also genuinely pretty proud of myself actually.

Holly reminds me that there's not a single other person even remotely like me, with even a fraction of my bravery, magic and love, and on my hard days, I remind myself I'm actually making a difference.

So, I'm living my happy ending: I don't want to die anymore. I have my moments occasionally, but I've overcome most of the bad stuff! I know I won't ever stop hurting but I'm ok. Still have the occasional nightmare, but otherwise I'm awesome.

No more trance states, no more yelling at strangers. No more drinking and climbing high things. I am perfectly happy and free. I am confident and strong and truly happy. People like me and I see it.

I am worthy and enough even on the bad days and I can promise myself, and those who care, all the tomorrows until God needs me back up there. Despite the difficult and disturbing events in this chapter, I really hope you feel moved and inspired!

If I can look the devil in the eyes and then crawl and fight my way back from the very deep depths of hell itself, I hope you realise you too have the strength to overcome and achieve anything!!

Also, just so you know, I left the worst and most horrible stories of the abuse out. I have the most terrifying, disgusting, haunting nightmares and memories. I don't think it's fair to burden you guys with those nightmares too. I gave you enough details so that others who have been horrifically hurt will know they aren't alone and to give the rest of you an idea of what goes on in the world. So maybe be more tolerant of others; you never know the burdens they carry. My part of this book was so hard to write and it almost shattered me. It took me ages because I could only face a few paragraphs at a time before I needed a break. It was a huge, heavy emotional strain. Editing Bunny and Holly's parts was a little easier.

Letting this go and leaving it behind me now, completely forgiving anyone and everyone who ever hurt me graciously with understanding and compassion.

Signing off to live happily (cheekily and naughtily) ever after.

Oodles of love,

Always and forever,

Your friend, *Kitten*.

Special thanks to:

(In no particular order)

My favourite high school teacher Mike, who even though I was a little tyrant, was mature enough to see through everything and not be mean like the other teachers, but actually try to help me. We are still close friends and he has been my rock writing this, constantly reminding me of my awesomeness, my bravery and also the importance and gravity of this novel. I am so grateful for you and your infinite support, babe. X

My lovely spanky Possum man.

A huge mountain of gratitude for Dr Anthony Markus, who has been the father I've always longed for, who actually cares about me in a fatherly way and proves this to me constantly. You gave the broken little girl in me the thing she always dreamed of and wanted most. Your love is slowly healing me. Thank you Daddy.

Hehe, I love saying that and calling you Daddy. It's not something I ever thought I'd ever get to say. I have never felt so completely at ease with anyone like I do with you. There are two people I sort of trust in this world: Holly and you. You are a truly remarkable human being and I'm so grateful God chose you to be my dad. It was definitely worth the wait. Every time you show me you care through your words, kind gestures and actions, one of my shattered puzzle pieces clicks into place. In the dark loneliness of night and my worst moments, when I'm struggling to breathe, it's you I turn to.

The son of Zeus, for saving my life, waking me up emotionally and giving me inspiration to dream and fantasize, you sexy boy.

My mum, who gave up everything after the accident to help me and did the best she was capable of, trying so hard for me always.

To my bestest friend ever Moodle, sweet, lovely and thoughtful, always there for me, making sure I smile and laugh every single day. Gives me the Koolest birthday cards.

To my goofball, who is a sweet, gentle man. For getting me through some really tough days with cuddles and laughter, you have this strange ability to brighten up my day and make the hard stuff easier.

My big brother, D. You walked into my life, grabbed a chair and sat down in my heart, like you belong there; you do. You light up my life and give me a safe space to be me. You have no idea how much you changed for me, but also within me. You made me feel. I love you Big Bro.

Of course my Bunny, Amy, who has always adored me, for thinking I'm a superhero and inspiring me, hosting the best all-girl sex parties. Also for giving me a kind of mother experience.

Lastly, but most importantly: a very special, deeply heartfelt thanks to my best friend, sidekick and soulmate, Miss Holly A, the robin to my batman (hehe…batkitten?) Thank you for fighting for me, for opening my eyes, for jumping into hell to pull me out again and again, for picking me up from the police station or hospital, or the floor and for not being too mad when I threw a plate that hit your face. For all our ridiculous adventures and every moment, good, bad, crazy and usually silly. You know you are my best friend and soulmate.

I am a giant and a superhero because you loved me and because you showed me how to love myself. You literally fought and worked persistently until you broke down the walls of the impenetrable prison I built around myself, helped me fight the demons within, set me free from the endless darkness and held my paw until I got reaccustomed to the light. 'Thank you' is not strong enough a sentiment.

So let me officially introduce you to Holly. Beautiful blonde/bronde, hot, fit, sporty bod, big boobs (YUMMY), smart, fun and one of the very few people who I've ever felt actually truly sees me, gets me, accepts and likes me.

She thinks she saw me first all those years ago in Surfers, but what she doesn't know is she parked near me. I watched her get out and followed her to cocktails and dreams. I was actually heading down to Melbas on Cavil, but the way her cute little butt shakes when she walks captured my attention, and I'm so glad it did.

Hol and I have the most insane connection and are incredibly close. She fought for me and refused to give up until I let her in. We are the very best of friends and I think she knows me better than I know myself. She is writing the second last chapter of this book. She is going to include stories from our life together, something a little lighter after the hard, dark stuff in my chapter!

Chapter Three

Holly

My friend, Kitten is the love of my life. I am Holly, her best friend and soulmate, by far her biggest fan. I will do my best to continue her conversational writing style. My side of her story is equally important because Kit will never let you see her true self. Partly because she hides it to protect herself, kind of like a turtle in its shell, but mainly because she doesn't see it.

Kit grew up believing that she was worthless, unwanted, unlovable not even likeable. I have tried so hard to change this and have never been able to completely budge it, but I very much want you to be able to see and understand the girl I love and her pure golden heart. I have seen Kitten at her absolute worst, but I've stuck by her side no matter how hard it got. I've followed and chased her into the darkness, not only in her mind but out into the actual night when she's had a meltdown/ trance. I've fought to bring her back from the brink of oblivion. I've seen looks of pain and horror so profound on her face that it makes every cell in my body hurt for her.

I've seen the way the world treats her: there are some people who are intimidated by, scared of and jealous of her power, magic, confidence, beauty, strength, etc! Yet I've seen her kindness and loving nature shine so many times in the face of all the bad, the hard and the unfair and that's the biggest thing I want to impart to you. It doesn't seem important to her because it comes so naturally. Anyone else subjected to what she has endured would be a serial killer, psychopath or mass murderer at the very least!! But she is the most remarkable girl I have ever met, quite possibly in existence. Yeah ok, I'm totally biased because I'm madly in love with her, but still. She is so compassionate, forgiving, understanding and caring.

I have not a shred of doubt she would take a bullet, give her life for a stranger, enemy, possibly even someone's pet. I can totally see her dashing into a burning building to save an animal when the firemen deem it unsafe. Probably cheekily yelling out, 'aww, grow some balls, boys,' as she did, or pulling someone from a burning car, even as her own skin caught fire. I've seen her give strangers money or food when she has not enough for herself. She once tried to get doctors to let her donate her organs while she was still alive. Her ridiculous yet somewhat still feasible argument was 'Well, the stuff I get myself into, I won't be alive much longer and I'll probably smash them so bad they won't be usable. This way I get to meet the people I'm saving'. The doctors obviously didn't let her, as she was still using them. I said to her, 'I can't believe they didn't lock you up in the psych ward.'

She replied, 'They were probably too scared to.' I imagine she was right.

Every year for her birthday, she does a charity thing. Saves up all year and gives it to people and animals in need. She once told me she has always felt like everyone's protector.

I can't imagine anyone else sacrificing themselves for others so many times the way Kit has, does and always will. There are times I've been brought to my knees by the unfairness of it all.

Kitten doesn't feel emotions because when she was little, she got to the point where she couldn't take the pain of constant neglect, abuse and rejection anymore, so she taught herself not to feel anything. The night she told me what happened to her and what those men did to her, I had streams of tears pouring down my face. She lay there, rigid and emotionless in my arms. I asked her why she never cries. She replied, 'I can't cry; they beat it out of me; I don't feel because I couldn't stand the pain anymore. I had to kill all emotions.'

I think over the years I have cried enough on her behalf to make up for the tears she can't shed. Kit and I are soulmates. We are best friends, twins, practically telepathic. We make deep intimate love, and we have passionate intellectual arguments, which she wins more often than not, Little Miss Smarty Pants. However, I know I will never get to keep her. We will always be together, in a spiritual way.

I pray she will find a man who will glue together her millions of shattered pieces. Kitten insists she needs to be alone and to be honest, that's understandable; then she can't get hurt anymore.

I live in constant fear of waking up to a world without Kitten. She is always falling off or out of something, or getting tangled in bungy jumping cord or parachutes while doing triple backflips, etc. Also, I can see her weariness and how much she craves peace. I've been in the bed beside her when she screams from her nightmare, 'Please, stop, it hurts so much,' or, 'don't hurt them; hurt me.' I have heard her scream unfathomably bone-chilling things from the depths of hell. I can't imagine how men could hurt little girls like that. Innocent children.

Kitten has woken my neighbours with screams for mercy. She's run out into the night in some sort of trance in an effort to escape the pain. But she can never get away from the memories within. She's yelled at strange men in clubs when drunk. She has drunk her way through the hardest days. She's cut, burnt and hurt herself when it got too much. She even asked me to kill her once when she was really struggling.

But she has this unique way of making everything in life better and is always getting into trouble somehow. She seriously gives new meaning to 'there's never a dull moment'. Her poor mum gets calls from the hospital at least once, but often more, every week. The police call me a couple times a month. It works well; sometimes the hospital calls me if they can't get hold of her mum.

Kitten has this kind of intense sexual swagger and she pours her raw sexuality over everyone she meets. It's so attractive and alluring that, coupled with her sweet affectionate caring nature, men often get the wrong impression. Even though she explains ad nauseam, they don't seem to get it. They are always trying to take advantage of her and pushing her.

Kitten has an irresistible sexual prowess and is very sexual in nature and personality, but she's not slutty.

Well, not normally. At a party once, I saw her get with three different girls in one night. But she was off her face, and they all had big boobs; Kit loves big boobs. So, you can't blame her … I'm a fairly large fan of big boobs myself, and really, in this day and age… who isn't?

I want to talk about Kit's sexuality. It was so hard for her to accept herself and her deeply sexual nature because of her childhood. She said it made her feel ashamed, disgusting and hate herself more. I showed her she is who she is in spite of, not because of, what happened to her, and it's the truth. This is one area where I really helped her accept, if not like herself and when she finally understood and did accept herself, her personality shone and she seemed freer and less tense. It was a pretty big fight, but now she accepts herself without hate. A big part of it is a coping mechanism for her; all her inappropriate jokes are her way of dealing with the heavy burden she carries alone, how she relieves some of the pressure and discomfort she feels having to be around men. It's really hard for her; especially strange men, and instead of being angry, bitter and difficult, she's a bit of a tease and makes inappropriate jokes.

They are funny, and most people laugh. Some don't understand and judge her, but to be blatantly honest, I don't think anyone would or could blame her if she snapped and started hitting men at random, with a sledgehammer.

Everyone she's ever met adores her, and if you get to know her and spend time with her, she imprints on your heart. You can't resist her cheekiness, that smile and her sweet affectionate loving ways.

It's October 2011.

I'm getting dressed to head into Surfers to go drinking and dancing. I chuck on a cute dress, do my hair and makeup without even the slightest clue I'm about to meet the smartest, most amazing loving girl to ever grace this earth. No idea the love of my life is getting ready and heading to the same club.

I drive in and park (total nightmare) and jump out and head towards the club. I'm standing outside having a smoke when I see a gorgeous blonde striding down the sidewalk, turning all heads as her high heels clack on the concrete, an air of strength and confidence surrounding her.

I watch transfixed as she scans the crowds. She looks in my direction and I glance away, focusing on a group of police standing to one side. As she struts past, one of them says, 'are you gonna behave tonight?'

A burst of sweet, cheeky laughter fills the air, and she grins and replies, 'Ha, in your dreeeaaamms, boys.'

I head into the club and grab a drink. It's summer, and it's hot and sweaty. I love the thick bass and head out to the dance floor, dropping into the zone immediately. After a while, I head to the bar for another drink.

Leaning against a concrete pillar, I survey the dance floor and spot a pair of pretty blue eyes locked on me, and a tiny thrill shoots through my veins as I realise it's the girl from outside. She smiles at me and I watch the dancers part for her. Like a goddess, she moves towards me.

All of a sudden, she's standing next to me. 'Hey beautiful,' she says, so cool, smooth and calm, inches from my face, looking directly into my eyes.

My 'hi' comes out as a tiny squeak. How embarrassing!

She giggles, puts an arm on the pillar and leans in, brushing her soft lips against mine. I am frozen in a hypnotic state, looking into her eyes. She makes me feel like I'm safe, like I'm home, like I've known her forever.

My heart is pounding wildly as she tilts my chin up and kisses me, softly and sweetly for a moment; then, when I kiss her back, our kiss deepens into passion, and we kiss for a long time, our hands and tongues exploring until some idiot boy yells out, 'OMG, there's two chicks going for it.' And whoops erupt from behind us.

She pulls back, grins at me, and then suggests we leave. Taking my hand, she leads me outside. 'I'm Bella,' she says as we step outside.

'Holly Andrea,' I reply and instantly feel stupid. I should have just said Holly. The cops are still standing around, and I catch them checking us out. She stops me and kisses me right there in front of everyone. I kiss her back, my head spinning. And my body hungry for hers. We then walk down to the beach where we sit and chat for a while; then we start making out and have fairly uncomfortable sandy sex. We are both drunk, it is hot and sweaty and we ended up looking like human schnitzels. So we go for a swim at 2 am and walked dripping wet, hand in paw back through Surfers to the cab rank.

The police are still patrolling Orchid Avenue and snort with laughter when they see us.

'One day we are going to have to arrest you girl.' She laughs. 'You already tried that, remember? I liked the cuffing part a bit too much.' She giggles. 'I don't think being extremely sexy is a crime boys. Sorry, not sorry!' I feel like I'm with a rock star.

I'm so smitten by her confidence and fun cheeky nature! I can't believe she chose me. I am the one who gives her the nickname Kitten. We are inseparable for the next six months, caught up in a dream of lovemaking, laughter, naughtiness and crazy fun. She really is like a rock star, hence the secondary nickname I give her, RocKIT, full of energy and vibrance. Everyone knows her name and loves her.

She had me completely fooled for a few months, but then I started to see cracks appear. Mainly when we were drinking, but sometimes just in the quiet moments of a regular day. Something overtook her, and if I was looking right at her, I swear I could see the colour drain from her face and light disappear from her eyes. It was like looking at someone in the very last moments before and as they died.

Her personality would shrink, then disappear and her eyes would become unfocused as she was pulled back in time to some horrible place that I later learned was 'the very depths of hell itself'.

One night when we are out in da club, some guy grabs her and is all over her. It didn't even occur to me that she might need my help. She'd never needed help with anything. But all of a sudden she's yelling and accusing the guy of wanting to rape her. I nearly drop my drink. I set it on the bar, push my way through the crowd. She has stopped yelling but is quietly losing it. She is wild-eyed and breathing so hard she is panting. I walk over, put my arms around her and try to calm her. She is rigid in my embrace. People are staring, but she didn't notice or care. I casually explain she's clearly had too much drink, as if people always start yelling 'rape' when drunk. We stand there for a few minutes; then I lead, or rather drag, a stone-like Kitten from the club. On the way out, she grabs one of the bouncers and dives into his arms, holding him tightly. He wraps his huge arms around her, holds her tight, and says, 'Are you ok, my sweet little darling?'

She is not ok; she is shaking in his arms. Apparently having witnessed the whole thing, he shoots me a questioning look, and I meet his concerned gaze and shrug, reaching over to stroke her hair. I won't lie; I am more than a little jealous she chose his arms over mine, but I realise that night there is something she isn't telling me. Something very dark and scary.

I had to fight to earn her trust over and over again. She would push me away. I'd give her space but never let it stick; I'd come right back by her side, proving to and showing her over and over that I was there and I truly cared about her. I know from my own life experience that people who have been badly hurt often need someone to fight for them and to prove themselves many, many times before they will start to trust. That was ok with me; I was happy to fight. Every minute with her was heaven.

We became more familiar, and she started to trust me, slowly. I saw it in little ways at first. She often went into that dark place, and I'd go wrap my arms around her, press my lips to her cheek, and try to lead her back to the light.

For a long time, she would push me away and walk off, disappearing for sometimes an hour but usually longer. After a while, I noticed she started pushing me off less forcefully and one day didn't push me off at all. She leant into me, defeated. I knew I'd finally won; all those months of fighting for her were worth it. She was finally starting to see.

The first time I told Kitten I loved her was the first time anyone had ever said those words to her. I didn't realise it at first; when I said it, her faced crumpled up like a hurt child about to burst into tears and she looked tortured, her eyes glistening with unshed tears. She said, 'Wait, what, really? Why?'

I replied, 'I love you because you're so amazing, Kitten.' Then she started thanking me profusely, which stunned and offended me for a few minutes, because I was hoping for 'I love you too'. She kept saying thank you over and over with such intense sincerity that eventually I realised why: I was the first person to ever care about her, and it was the first time she had ever heard those words. A similar thing happened when a stranger called her gorgeous; she was so grateful. I can't believe she got to almost 20 years old without ever being told she was loved or pretty.

One night in my living room on Chevron, we are cuddling, having just finished making love. All of a sudden I notice her breathing change and her body go rigid in my arms. I sit up and pull her into my lap so I can see her face properly. I watch her light fade and eyes get unfocused.

'Kit honey,' I say softly as I smooth her hair from her face. 'When are you going to tell me what haunts you?' She takes a deep breath and sighs loudly, telling me in a small, embarrassed voice, 'Never, because it's unfair to burden anyone else with that story and you will hate me.'

I lean down and kiss her forehead. 'RocKIT, I love you higher than the sky and deeper than the ocean. I could never hate you.' I look down at her gorgeous pixie face and remembered the look of torment she gets. I gently push her.

'Please tell me. I want to be able to understand so I can help.'

Lying there in my lap, Kit started telling me of her childhood and how she felt unlovable, unlikable, unwanted, was barely fed, touched, or even acknowledged and was always alone. Tears started to pour down my face as she told me of the paedophile ring that abused her, the nine different men that raped, tortured, beat and did horrible things to her. Her face was distorted with pain and horror. Once she started, she told me the whole story. I look at her hands; they are clenched and completely white from the pressure. A few of my tears drip on her and she twists in my lap, wiping the tears away with a fingertip. She says, 'Don't cry for me; I'm already dead' and continued on telling me everything with that look of horror and pain distorting her gorgeous face. Rage coursed through me as she told me the worst of it. I can't imagine how it must have felt for her as a child. She told me about the toothbrush case incident and a few significantly worse stories. I feel really sick and let out a little burp. She says, 'I'm ok with a tear on me. Not so much puke Hol.'

I hastily push her off, jump up, and run to the bathroom to be sick. When I get back, Kitten is lying on the floor in the same position I left her. I bend down and lift her up. I spin her around and looking into her eyes, tell her I love her. That was the moment I realised I had glimpsed the real Kitten, a tiny little girl being hurt so badly and so very desperate for love, attention and affection.

I suspect that the reason she's always felt so separate and disliked is most likely because, even as a little child, Kitten's intelligence, maturity, vibrance and unique, gregarious nature probably intimidated people. A small child smarter and more mature than most adults would certainly set many people offside and this is undoubtedly the reason why she felt no one liked her. She is so magnificent and exceptional, in a galaxy of her own. She kind of does speak a different language, her own, 'Kittenish', maybe, haha.

I was looking right at her the first time it happened. I guess talking about it triggered the intense trance states. I was the first person she told the whole entire story to. Kitten and I have the connection and love that everyone searches for. We are always all over each other, can't touch, kiss, be close enough. I was always there for her through it all; it was me who pointed out, then painstakingly convinced her, that some people treat her the way they do because they are jealous, and they are. She's always so confidently and unabashedly herself.

There are people who fall in love with her and go batshit crazy when she isn't interested. Some of them stalk, are mean to and harass her. You wouldn't believe the lengths some of them go to, trying to get her attention. Even though she explains to everyone repeatedly, very clearly, and in no uncertain terms: that she is flirty and has an inappropriate sense of humour, but there's no interest or invitation from her; that she is affectionate, loving, caring and kind; not to take it personally, she's the same with everyone and in a committed relationship. She tells most men she is gay. Nevertheless, both men and women go apocalyptic. I reckon sewer rat is one of them.

I often take her face in my hands, kiss her softly and look into her eyes, reminding her that some people feel small, insignificant and insufficient standing next to a giant. But the day it first happened was shortly after she told me. I am looking into her pretty blue eyes and reminding her of her importance and place in the world when all of a sudden she turns stiff and white, her eyes become unfocused, and she stares into the distance beyond my shoulder. Her face distorts in horror for a second. I have no idea what's happening. I glance over my shoulder quickly, half expecting to see something terrible, afraid to look away for too long, I look back at her and realise she's being sucked away to some different time and place to some horrible memory. She starts shaking, and her eyes fill with sad water that doesn't escape. She whispers, barely audibly, 'Please stop; it hurts so bad.'

I knew instantly where she was. 'Kitten, baby?' I call her name, nothing, she whimpers softly. Her pupils are so small, I realise suddenly that I am losing her to the darkness. Fear rips through my insides.

'Kitten!' I scream and violently shake her. There is no change, so I lean forward and brush my lips against hers, saying, 'I love you.' Just in case she isn't coming back, I want her to hear it one last time.

She snaps out of it, looks at me, and asks me, 'What happened?' But I have neither idea nor answer. This happens more and more. The first few times she comes back quickly and easily, but as it continues, it gets harder to bring her back and sometimes she is different. We soon realise there is a very real danger we could lose her completely to the darkness within.

And this was the exact moment I saw through her act. I watched the shutters come down and the facade back up. She took a breath and put on her fake smile, and more despair flooded me as I realised the vast depths of her agony.

I became more determined than ever to fight for her and help her, to love her pain away like she does for everyone else. Most of the people who are in our friend group are people she has helped. Bella literally reaches out to everyone and tries to help, inspire and build them up and she always succeeds. She fixed Amy, and trust me, that was a hell of a job.

A lot of people stay in her life; she's so awesome to be around, such a good loyal friend. Also wicked crazy fun and exciting, she talks like she writes. She is interesting, captivating and enthralling even in normal, regular conversation. She often inadvertently attracts a crowd and audience when telling stories or just talking loudly in public.

One night we are walking along the esplanade and come across a drunk guy in a wheelchair crying and reeking of pee. A group of people are watching with looks of pity from a safe distance.

I hear her mutter, 'people are so mean,' and she skips from my side over to him, puts a paw on his shaking shoulder, and says, 'Hey cutie pie, are you ok?' He responded with a suspiciously wet-sounding fart and a sound that resembled a horse snorting. Everyone took a step back except Kitten, who takes a step forward and wrapped her arms around his shuddering body. He stills for a moment, then lets out a howl of pain and a loud sniff and stuttered something about his girlfriend leaving him.

I could smell an intense mixture of poo, urine and sweat, and I am two metres away. My eyes watered, but Kit says something I'll never forget. She holds him tighter and says, 'Yeah babe, bitches be crazy!' There is a snicker from the bystanders, and I smile a bit through the tears that are pouring down my cheeks as I listen to her console him and tell him he is handsome and sweet and he'll find someone even better soon.

I watch her and feel my own heart breaking, seeing this girl who had been hurt so badly, deeply and irrevocably, and here she was, the heroine yet again, oozing love for a stranger in need when she couldn't even manage to like herself.

As usual, it was Kitten who stepped up and behaved appropriately while the rest of the world stood by gawking. I feel a rush of love for her; admix with sadness at how unfair life is. As she stands there, her paw on his shoulder, I realise I want to spend my life with her. I want to be there for her every time she gets lost or sad, like she is for everyone else: friend, stranger, enemy.

Kitten deserved to be taken care of, there are many nights where she wakes covered in sweat, pleading for mercy or screaming, 'Please stop. It hurts so much,' or, 'Please don't hurt them; hurt me.' Then she does her trance-state walk, out into the darkness.

One night, she kicks me hard, screams something unintelligible, jumps up and flies out the door stark naked into the chilly winter night. I get up; half throw on some pyjamas and go after her. Normally she walks slowly in her trance state, but this time she ran. I couldn't find her until I heard excited male voices, then whistling. OMG. Fear tears through me. I move closer to their voices, what am I going to do? What would Kitten do!? I am a petite blonde; the male voices sounded big and tough. Could I call the cops? Was there time? There wasn't time; it'd be too late.

A horrible feeling dawned on me. If I don't do something right now, Kitten was going to get hurt badly, probably raped again.

I muster up bravado I don't feel, mixed with anger and adrenaline pulsing through my veins. I put on my best gruff voice, which in all honesty wasn't gruff at all.

I sound like a drunk American. I yell, 'Oi, you dickheads, stay away from my girl.

If you so much as touch her with one finger, I will skin the sack off your balls and make you eat it with the eyeballs I rip outta of your skulls. Now back the hell up, turn around AND RUN! Because if I catch you, I'm going to kill you slowly.'

I'm pretty impressed with my own on-the-spot creativity. I strain my ears and hear footsteps retreating. I wait till the sound fades a bit because if they see me, a barely dressed female, we might both get hurt. Then I run around to find my naked Kitten in a tiny ball on the icy ground. 'Baby, baby, are you ok?' I pull her to her feet. She looks at me and she smiles. 'Skin the sack from your balls,' she repeats. I burst out in laughter, mainly in relief I think and to my surprise, Kit kind of joins in. She is still smiling.

We can only assume that imminent danger somehow almost broke her trance state but I still don't think she was aware enough to protect herself, only to recognise my voice. We stand there in the dewy grass for a while; then her mood turns sombre and sad and I poke her belly and say, 'You're going to have to start sleeping in snow gear and a chastity belt.'

'You're going to have to start tying me to the bed,' she replies. I raise my eyebrows at her and giggle 'maybe we should go practice that.'

So we walk, me half dressed in pyjamas, and Kitten naked, back to my place hand in paw. What a peculiar sight that would have been.

One night, my ex-girlfriend, who is a nasty whore, is having a party. She'd been spreading BS rumours about me. I ask my gorgeous blonde kitten to come as my sidekick and let me show her off. We decide to walk, it isn't far. We get all glammed up and we both look so gorgeous - some poor person has a minor car accident watching us as we kiss. We are half-way there when Kitten orders me to stop and be quiet. I look over her shoulder.

There is a little boy sitting there all alone in the cold winter darkness in nothing but a T-shirt and shorts, arms wrapped around his knees. I step back and Kitten goes over and says, 'Hey kiddo, are you alright?' He looks up wearily and tells her to F off. She doesn't, she gently pulls him to his feet.

'It's ok. I'm a good stranger; you can trust me. Whatcha doing out here all by yourself so late?' He umms and ahs, looking at his shoes. She steps forward and wraps her arms around him, saying, 'You're safe, kid. I got ya.' To my amusement and her surprise, he rubs his face in her boobs. 'Argh.' She jumps back in disgust and says, 'Wait here with my friend one sec,' and grabs me so I go next to the kid, 'Jack'. He looks slightly familiar, but I can't place it. Kitten goes a little way off and I see she's on her phone. I look at him wearily. 'Sup, dude,' is all I could think to say. He looks so lost. Kit comes back and orders him not to move a muscle. He nods without speaking. She pulls me away and says, 'Someone's hurting that kid. Police are on their way.'

'The party,' I mutter, my spirits sinking, but I already know we aren't going, and I know she is right. You can see it on his little face, the same undercurrent of torment, pain and fear I've seen on her face at times. She takes off her jacket, wrapping him in it and puts her arms around his little body, saying, 'Kiddo, it's ok. I gotcha, you're safe now. Everything's gonna be just fine.' He leans into her, grips her tightly and starts to cry so hard he chokes.

I watch, unsure of what to do, but eventually I go and stroke his hair, then wrap my arms around them both.

Finally the cops pull up. They are too by the book and reprimand us for hugging the boy. I see them running their eyes over Kitten's body. She starts to explain, but the officer won't listen, his eyes glued to her tits. She pushes Jack into my arms, turns to the officer, takes his hand and leads him away a bit, but I still hear what she's saying, explaining the boy shows classical signs of serious child abuse and asking him politely to look into it. He basically tells her to mind her own business; then, she grabs him forcefully by the front of the shirt and says, 'Ok, listen up, you arrogant idiot.

I spent my childhood being hurt. There is no justice for me. I'm a counsellor, and I can tell 100% that kid is being abused, not just neglected. He is being hurt badly, so here's what's gonna happen. You're going to look into it. You're going to stop it, or I swear, if you don't, I will go to the media with a story about how you personally failed to help a child being hurt. Got it?'

His partner was moving forward menacingly. 'Kitten!' I get her attention and nod towards the other guy. 'Oh, keep your pants on. We are just talking!' she yells.

I laugh so hard I snort loudly, like a horse. Then it made me laugh harder and I couldn't stop. You know, like when you're a kid and you really need to stop but it just makes it worse, Jack thinks my snorting is funny and laughs too. Kitten is glaring at us furiously; that sobers me up real fast.

'So listen boys, the kid is coming home with us tonight and until you have a chance to investigate and find somewhere safe for him.' She says it in a tone of finality that allowed neither argument nor discussion. The older officer opened his mouth to say something, but Kitten shoots him a look so poisonous he shuts it instantly. Neither of the policemen argue. I look at skinny little Jack and say, 'How does that sound? I could go for a pizza?' We give them my number and walk off with Jack, who is thrilled by my offer of pizza. (He wolfs down an entire pizza himself, plus garlic bread and dessert.) The relief on his face makes my heart swell with pride and affection for my Angel.

This night was a turning point: a new improved Kitten emerged, even more confidant, strong and proud. Seeing her like that, I could unquestionably see her in her role as everyone's protector. In a strange twist of fate, Jack turns out to be Amy's little brother, who had been sent to a foster home years ago when Amy's parents walked off and left him alone at the beach. He almost drowned. His foster parents were not very attentive and let his foster siblings beat, torment and abuse him. We keep Jack safe with us for a bit over a week. Kit works hard to earn his trust with patience, reassurance and kindness. After a couple of days, the sullen, angry, scared little boy was giggling.

We spoil him rotten, buy him nice new clothes, some boy toys, take him to Timezone and feed him properly. He loves it. We give him lots of hugs and safe affection. With her gentle persistent love, he finally opens up and tells her what was happening to him and she told the police. Jack's foster parents are arrested and the police want to give Kitten some sort of official hero commendation (not just for this, in recognition of everything she does), but she thanks them and humbly refuses.

She really struggles with accepting compliments, praise and accolades. It's so alien to her; she has no idea how to respond. She says, successfully saving him is enough. She kept in touch with Jack and counselled him over the years.

He is now a strapping grown-up with a family of his own. He is so grateful for our help and I love to watch them together. They have a strong bond. She still calls him 'little man'. He wraps his big bear arms around her, and tears roll down his face. I get choked up watching them.

Kitten's new confidence stayed after the night she saved Jack. It's funny to watch her in action because she's so little, pretty and dresses like a sex siren seductress. Men think they can walk all over her; then she opens her mouth and I love to watch them scuttle around like she's the queen. RocKIT doesn't take crap from anyone anymore. She knows her worth. She's very protective of everyone, children especially. If we come across one alone, we find their mum and dad or watch over them until the police come. Occasionally we would remove and protect an abused child from a bad situation like we did with Jack.

One day, Kit is helping me cook. She is chopping onions for me and I glance at her when she starts sounding sniffly. I suggest sunglasses to stop her crying. She throws down the knife and onion, looks at me fearfully and shrieks, 'I'm not crying. I'm NOT crying. My eyes are watering. I can't help it, I SWEAR,' then bolts from the room. I find her in the living room in a trembling ball, biting her lip hard. Her fists are clenched and knuckles white. 'I swear I wasn't crying!' she whispers hoarsely and flinches hard when I step forward.

I sink down behind her and pull her into my arms. I hold her tight and say something I'd heard her say to an abused child once. 'Sweetheart, you can relax. You're safe here. Safe to be yourself in every way, no one will hurt you here. There is nothing you can't say or do.' Then I stroke her hair and pull her rigid body into mine as close possible. I can feel her heart beating madly. She is breathing so hard I'm scared she might pass out; every muscle in her body is tensed into concrete. I tell her she is allowed to cry and remind her she is a grown up and those men can't hurt her anymore.

I have watched her constantly looking over her shoulder, flinching and getting terrified and angry if any strange men got too close or touched her. I've watched her lose control sometimes and yell at strange men. She punched one in the face once when he groped her. I almost hit him too; he was just a drunk idiot who groped a pretty girl and then he was a drunk idiot with a black eye. I don't think she meant to hit him, it was a reflex movement. She felt bad and apologized.

I keep telling Kitten she is safe and loved, over and over until Amy walks into the room. It took her a minute to realise what was happening and see Kitten's white face. Then she comes over and sits with us and starts singing Sexy Back - poorly. Then she takes one of Kit's paws in her hand and holds it while stroking her face. Nothing is working. I was thinking of calling an ambulance. I tell Amy to switch positions with me and I lift her chin, look into her eyes and tell her I love her. It always got her attention, I suspect because she never heard those words until we were together. I just say the words over and over. Amy sings Sexy Back louder. Nothing is working.

All of a sudden, she jumps in our arms and says something that still rips at my insides in the silent moments: 'I'm sorry; please don't hurt me. I didn't mean to cry. I get so scared when I see the knives. They hurt the worst and I'm scared I'm going to die.' She blurts it out quickly in a rush of words. Shaking even harder, teeth chattering wildly. Once again I realise I wasn't holding an adult. I'm holding the little girl who was about to be badly hurt, who was terrified, alone and hurting.

Amy meets my eyes, and I saw a maturity she didn't quite possess yet, but she finally understood. Her lip starts to tremble. I shake my head, silently pleading, 'Don't cry, we have to save Kitten!' I watch her eyes fill with tears and she tries to fight it but fails, and soon she is crying hard. But something amazing happens. Kit comes back with a sudden violent jolt, like she is re-entering her body at speed. Her voice is shaking, but she says, 'Bunny, sweetheart, why are you crying? What's wrong, babe?' using her thumb to wipe the tears that were flowing rapidly down Amy's sweet face.

I felt like she'd slapped me in the face. I wanted to cry myself, and I did later in private. Kit and I are soulmates, best friends and have the deepest connection. We say 'I love you' and we make love, but I know she doesn't feel love or have any romantic feelings for me, or anyone. It always hurts to see her intimate with anyone else in any way. Bunny and Kitten have a special bond. Amy's parents don't love her either and Amy is like her little sister. But I see the way they look at each other. There's more than just friendship and shared hurt; there's attraction and even though it upsets me, I'm happy for them. I want more than Kit can give me.

Well, so now I feel like I'm dealing with two children. Except I look at them and they're looking into each other's eyes, their faces so close. Kit says, 'So I guess now you know. Do you hate me and think I'm disgusting?'

'Of course not honey,' Amy reassures her. Tears coming fast again. 'You're perfect,' she whispers. We've all seen Amy's feelings for Kitten and I know what's coming. I want to scream and yell and let out all my frustration. But it doesn't last long because I know it's not Kitten's fault; I know she cares about me as much as she is capable of intimately caring about anyone.

I know we will always be together, and I think about what she said about the knives and my heart breaks. I smooth her hair, and I get up and leave to give them some privacy. I glance back to see them kissing, and you know, as angry and jealous as I am, my heart swells with pride. There is apparently literally nothing that will stop Kitten from helping someone else. I'm glad I now have another way to reach her in the darkness.

Amy buys Kitten a plate, some random thing they saw together at the markets. It's a nice plate, and Kit loves it. I lose my temper. I'm not proud, but I'm only human. Watching her make out with Amy wasn't fun; watching them all lovey-dovey and close hurt like hell. And now they were buying presents for each other. Kit and I have a huge fight. There is screaming and she shouts at me, 'It's just a freaking plate. If you hate it so much I'll smash it.'

She is genuinely getting very stressed and I'm suddenly afraid of what it might trigger, so I backtrack as fast as I can, but it isn't working.

Every time she goes back to hell, into the darkness, into one of those trance states, I'm terrified she won't come back the same, or she won't come back at all.

I couldn't live with myself if it was my fault. So I tried to clown around a bit. I went to do a dramatic side-step to make her laugh. I see the plate leave her hand a fraction too late and step directly into its flight path, intercepting its journey to the wall. It hits me right in the face. Kitten is at my side instantly apologising profusely, then cracks up laughing. I laugh with her.

She pins me down and tells me I'd always be number one. I remind myself that she doesn't feel emotions like everyone else. She cares deeply for everyone but when it comes to real personal emotions, attractions and feelings, she can't manage it at all after her childhood. I do understand and looking into her eyes it reminds me how lucky I am. I know she adores me deep down in some part beneath all the hurt and damage and I see it in her eyes. I know if things were different, if she could love, it would be me she'd choose.

The plate is broken so I go and buy a new one. For the first time ever, I have to share my Kitten. But they have a lot of fun and it makes me happy. I know Bunny cares about her like I do.

When Kit told me she'd started this book and her intentions of being honest, I was scared of what it might do to her. I watched her come undone and how much it hurt her, but she insisted her sacrifice was worth it; to help and inspire others!

Oh my love, you are so amazing, unique, and special.

There is a happy ending, of course; a few months ago Kitten asked me out on a romantic date night. She takes me to our fave restaurant and then to Surfers to where we first met. She takes me to the spot where I stood when I first saw her and she tells me, 'I know you think you saw me first, but I followed you from your car. I saw you get out and your cute little ass shake, your hot bod and those big boobs, and

I followed you. I was going to go to Melbas; then I saw you. I had to have you, you sexy thang.' She gets down on one knee and says, 'Holly Andrea, will you marry me?'

My heart bursts into butterflies, and for a second I think I'm dreaming. 'Yes, yes,' I practically yell, pulling her up. Then I go, 'Oh, wait. Haha, maybe. I'll think about it,' coolly and we both laugh and she looks into my eyes, says, 'I love you,' and we kiss. We have an intimate wedding with our closest friends and, of course, hot strippers with big tits.

Then we run away to our own secret honeymoon where we make love constantly and Kitten teases the concierge boys and waiters with fake invites to a threesome. We reminisce about all our crazy fun, good times, fantastic times and the day she threw a plate that hit me in the face.

We drink, we laugh, we make love, and we get melted chocolate everywhere and are told several times by management that we are disturbing the other guests. It is the most fabulous time of my life; I've never felt closer to or been more in love than with my Kitten. I can't shake a forlorn weight in my tummy though.

One night she wakes me, screaming for mercy, literally screaming too, not just words but blood-boiling screams of pain. She's back there. I act immediately and thankfully she's back quickly, sort of. She just lies there, panting. We are lying on our sides, looking into each other's eyes. She looks like a kitten in headlights, her eyes wide and fearful and she whispers, 'Please stop. It hurts so much. Make them stop.' Her eyes are watering and she's shaking and drooling and hyperventilating, very much like a severe seizure. There are stories of things that happened to her that aren't in this book; they are far too disgusting, violent, disturbing and absolutely frigging terrifying. There are things she can't and won't even tell me. She can't bear to put them into words and relive it. It would be the end of her sanity.

I lie there looking at her traumatised face, and I wish so hard, I beg God in my mind to take away her pain, even if it meant losing her memory. To see someone you love twisted in such extreme pain because of a memory is so hard. I have no idea how to help her or make it stop.

Another night, Kitten has a bad night episode, and I'm scared of her running out into the night again, so I climb on top of my thrashing, yelling girl and use my body to pin her down. I put my lips to her ear and I say, 'Come back to me, Kitten. I'm right here, never leaving your side. If you can't find a way out of the darkness, I'll come in and live there with you. I will help you fight over and over. I will follow you into hell again and again, I'm never giving up on you'. I push her hair from her sweaty face and tell her over and over that I love her and I'm never leaving. To the best of my knowledge, this is the last time she ever had a night incident. It wasn't just me; I think getting most of it out in this book helped.

But eventually, after almost a decade of fighting, we start to win a little. The trances get less severe and less frequent, and Kit starts to recognise her awesomeness. We are finally winning; she even stops trying to kill herself!

Then some low class, absolute piece of trash massage loser (rat) almost completely destroys this and the years of hard work by Amy and I, building her up and fighting for her. He is extremely lucky Kit doesn't like or allow violence and retaliation, or he'd be bloody dead. The worst part is: I know that even as he was abusing, hurting and tormenting her, she was caring about, being kind to and trying to help and heal him. Herein lies the unique beauty and indomitable, unfaltering majesty of her pure divine heart. It makes me cry angry, sorrowful tears. I know that would have been so very hard, terrifying, and retraumatizing for her. Trapped alone with a strange man and predator, being abused again. No wonder she fell apart. We hated watching her suffer so badly after him. There were a few really bad sleepless months where we were sure she was going to end her life.

But then she meets the son of Zeus, Dr Anthony, some random fireman and later her big brother, who change everything. I'm mad and hurt for roughly 20.5 seconds and then I'm elated that this has happened. Kitten smiles brightly as she tells us the stories, full of joy and animation.

I kinda hate the fireman because of the way he treated her, but it doesn't matter because between the five of us and her big bro, we set her free.

Y'all got to join us on this weird crazy rollercoaster adventure of saving my friend, Kitten.

Imagine, for a second, being a tiny baby, then a small child, that no one ever touches, hugs, holds or plays with. No one even looks or smiles at or says anything nice to, barely feeds and just treats badly. Then imagine being used by a paedophile ring as that same little child, passed around like you don't matter. Tortured, beaten, abused, used and injured for fun.

Imagine the hurt, the pain, the sadness, despair and the anger. What sort of person would that child grow up into? A psychopath, druggie and violent, messed-up person at the very least. That little girl was Kitten.

Look how she rose above it all, with no bitterness or pathology, just love, kindness and understanding.

I can see her as a little girl, colouring in her own version and idea of colours and I bet the picture looked better her way.

If someone told her to colour inside the lines, she wouldn't have, not because she couldn't, but because she didn't want to and hates being told what to do. My sweet little Angel is that one in a million, except that's not quite accurate! One in existence: a genuine renegade. She has her own completely unique charisma, panache and je ne sais quoi. She does, says and wears what she wants with class, elegance and style. She is a leader and trendsetter; people copy her. I hope lots of people copy her behaviour and kind loving ways after reading this!

Chapter Four

Counselling/Bonus Chapter

IMPORTANT NOTE/Disclaimer: Absolutely none of the information in this chapter is intended to be used to help or treat yourself or others. <u>Always seek advice and supervision from a trained, licensed professional</u>. The potential to misunderstand, misinterpret or misuse information and techniques outlined below could potentially result in endangering your own life and safety and the lives and safety of others.

I run my counselling business a little differently. I base my out-of-the-box, unique and extremely effective counselling methods on the premise that love heals and transcends everything. I have adapted play therapy, predominantly used to treat children, for use with adults. So, I call my business 'my friend' and the foundation behind it is that you hire me to be your friend and this gives me more autonomy treating people. I get creative, and I rarely use a clinical setting. We go for a walk along the beach or in the park and chat like friends. I do most things a friend would and this is why I'm immensely successful: because I get real, permanent results as you are relaxed, at ease, feel safe and have a caring friend helping you.

Generally speaking, you only need 1 to 4 sessions with me as opposed to 7 to 10 with a regular counsellor. I am appropriately affectionate when needed, I hug my clients too or hold their hand while they talk.

Ok guys, here is the bonus chapter, as promised. Let's start with you, the reader. You have to relearn to look within, heal yourself, cultivate the ability to listen, think, respond and act like a mature adult. You are completely perfect in every way.

You are loved, adored, worthy, enough. Right now, exactly as you are, on your good days/bad days/worst days, you are still perfect. We all must relearn to love and accept ourselves. We are conditioned by society to move away from love and self-love/acceptance, but the truth is there is no happiness without loving and accepting yourself. You are awesome; give yourself permission to see it. Some days you will do great; others, you'll barely make it out of bed, and that's ok. It's just being human. Be gentle, loving and understanding towards yourself. Take care of yourself and always put yourself first. You can't give to or help others if you are empty. It's you first, it's the only way.

Write yourself a letter about how great you are, how talented, beautiful, loveable, etc. On your hardest days, read it. Look in the mirror and tell yourself, I love you. I am so very proud of you. You are incredible. Then also say, I'm sorry for all the times I failed to be true to you and I forgive you for any times you weren't your best or made the wrong decision, did the wrong thing, etc. I understand you and I love you. Thank you for being you. Strive for your dreams, do what makes you happy, don't dwell on the past, look forward and stride confidently into the future.

Then turn these same ideals outward; love, accept and be forgiving and understanding of and with everyone. We are all human and therefore connected; everyone is doing their best, just as you are. Everyone makes mistakes, just as you do. Do not under any circumstances care what others think. Yours is the only opinion that matters. You have to be ready and willing to heal yourself. People can help you, but it starts with you. The power, the answers, are within you.

Inner child reconnection and healing exercise

Get a picture of yourself as a child or hold on to a memory you have of how you looked then. Sit in front of the mirror and gently request that your inner child come forth and join you. Look at yourself both now and then and say, hello, sweetheart. I love you and I've missed you! Thank you for joining me today. There are some things you need to understand. You are perfect, always have been and always will be. There are some things that have happened, are happening, and will happen to you, but you must know it's not your fault when other people behave badly. I'm sorry I couldn't explain this to you sooner, and I'm sorry if your feelings got hurt, but you need to know the way other people treat you is a reflection of them, not you. I know you try your best every day. I'm sorry if I ever got impatient or angry at you for things you didn't understand. You are remarkable and amazing. Everyone makes mistakes; it's normal. I'm sorry for all the times you felt confused, lost, or scared. That was my fault. I'm sorry for the times I should have protected you better but didn't or couldn't.

I want you to know I'm your biggest fan, and I'll always be right here by your side, cheering you on or fighting for you. Whatever is required, I'll always have your back. Please forgive me for the times I failed you. I forgive you for all the little mistakes you made and the times you weren't at your best. I adore you so much.

Imagine taking that little innocent child into your arms and holding them tight. Say, I love you, just as you are. Now, let's release all the past anger, bad feelings, guilt and sadness together. I will protect you; you can trust me. I do this much better and in depth in one-on-one sessions, but it's a start. Go for it. You can get creative and add anything you think your inner child needs to hear. Have fun with it.

Most people who have become psychopaths, monsters and abusers are primarily people who have experienced immense and depraved trauma and were not helped, cared about or counselled. The human psyche reaches a tipping point of how much pain and trauma it can handle alone, consequently; personalities fracture and splinter, becoming unstable and causing people to lose control of themselves and their behaviour, often resulting in psychosis and pathology. I believe theoretically, in most cases, this damage can be undone with love, understanding and proper support: you heal the original pain and trauma and the monster disappears. Similarly with bullies and really mean unhinged people. However, there is an innate opposite here, where some people are just born evil. This needs to be discerned on a case-by-case basis, with in-depth psychological analysis. Nevertheless, the majority of the time, massive unbearable emotional and psychological pain and horrible life experiences are to blame. Angry, hurting people lash out and hurt others, usually out of sheer desperation; they are screaming for help.

You hear stories about kids shooting up schools in America. They are usually deeply hurting, lashing out and desperate for love, attention and help. It's so sad that it comes to this, those kids would show lesser signs of not coping with trauma long before they pick up a gun, if someone recognizes this and helps them then there is no resorting to a gun! This is a big part of why I'm trying to educate and reunite everyone. If we start paying more attention and learning to recognize certain behaviours, then learning/understanding how to help people… helping and providing them with loving, understanding support, we can heal <u>EVERYONE</u>.

What a loving, peaceful world that would be!! I truly understand/know/believe that love can heal and transcend everything. This is also why I was able to forgive those men. I understand *everything*.

Helping others

Most importantly, the largest part of helping people includes reading between the lines of their behaviour and thinking about the reasons behind their behaviour, then addressing the causal/ underlying issues. Remember, hurt/ hurting people lash out and hurt others. Just showing caring attention and listening will go a long way to helping anyone and everyone. Love is the answer. Hug them, include them, and accept them.

If you are dealing with someone who has turned to alcohol or drugs, the best way to get them off is slowly. Distraction helps and this works with other things like anxiety and depression, even suicidal tendencies because you're rewiring the brain. If they're in deep and need to detox, it's messy and nasty, sweaty and gross for a while, but when the worst is over, it's the best thing ever. They are so grateful.

Even if they aren't in detox, when their body starts craving and demanding drugs or alcohol, use yummy food and other pleasurable experiences: yes sex, and mainly affection, fun activities like shopping, but especially sports and physical activities. Even a swim at the beach, walk in the park, or taking them to a candy or cake shop and going crazy.

Start with the really good things like yummy food and sex/masturbation (these have the greatest impact on the pleasure centres in the brain). Essentially, you're rewiring their brain to crave nice things like yummy food etc. in place of drugs and alcohol. You will be surprised how quickly it works, and you will see differences and improvements after the 3rd or 4th time, eventually you can safely and effectively get them/yourself clean completely and/or get rid of anxiety, depression and suicidal thoughts. You may need a doctor if withdrawal symptoms are severe, but don't let it discourage you. It will pass, be strong.

It's <u>IMPERATIVE you watch them closely</u> and talk often about their feelings and if they are coping. Especially if suicidal thoughts are present.

I refuse to work by Zoom or the internet for most clients because suicidal thoughts are a tough one. Usually if they are telling you, it's because they want help. But not always! Giving their possessions away is a huge warning sign though. I can't elaborate on this further; I fear putting someone at risk. If there's a medical problem, unstable or violent behaviour or you suspect there's a suicide possibility call an ambulance for them right away.

At the end of the day, loving someone, listening, and genuinely caring for someone is all it really takes. So many people feel alone, unwanted and unloved. Just stepping up and being there and actively listening will start to heal hurting people.

Sometimes when people are hurting really badly, they get caught up in their pain and they won't/can't hear you. This happens predominantly in people with depression, anxiety, suicidal tendencies and other emotional problems. All you can really do is be there for them, remind them that they are important, loved, and adored. Also that they are strong and will get through this and that the feelings will pass. As hard as it seems at the time, the feelings usually do pass.

Try pleasurable distraction techniques, and if they are not responding or have suicidal thoughts, seek immediate help. In extreme cases, call an ambulance if you think there is danger that they may injure themselves or take their own life.

Self-harm is usually an attempt to get a break from intense psychological, mental and emotional pain by moving it to the physical. Many people physically injure themselves to get a break from the incredibly intense pain they feel inside and the turmoil in their head. Having done this myself, I know exactly how effective it is - and it truly is. It works instantly, yet the relief is short lived. Or it's someone punishing themselves. If working with or if you know someone who self-harms, get them to communicate when the pain is getting too heavy to carry alone. Talk to them about what they are thinking/feeling and employ distraction techniques as I outlined earlier: fun physical activities, journaling, affection, shopping, good food, pleasurable activities that rewire the brain and serve as a reminder it's not all bad. Self-harm is often linked to suicidal thoughts, so make sure you seek professional support. Do not judge or treat them differently; this is the worst thing you can do. Pull them closer, hug them, care. If there's another human being hurting this bad, step up and help!

I have a very close friend who has an abusive, narcissistic parent and suffers from emotional and social problems as a result. Although I've offered to work with him, both alone and with his family, he refuses. So when he texts me that he just wants to die, I reply with how much I love him, how important he is, and that it will pass. Then send funny memes.

All mentions of suicide like this should be taken VERY SERIOUSLY. Stay with them all night if you have to. Sometimes though, people who are hurting really badly just need you to be there for and with them through the toughest parts. They need to know they matter and someone cares, and that's all you need to do. Although I don't believe my friend will take his own life, if I can't get to him, I reach out to family members or other friends and colleagues just letting them know to be more supportive, loving and closely watchful.

Abuse

Signs of sexual abuse in children can include:

* Social withdrawal or sudden quietness, wanting to be alone, elective mutism

* Bed wetting and or soiling themselves especially in older children

* Sudden strange attention-seeking behaviour

* Sexual behaviour, especially open sexual behaviour (e.g. inappropriately touching themselves, others or asking sexual questions, mimicking sexual acts)

* Sudden bouts of unexplained anger and irritability

* Inability or unwillingness to make eye contact

* Fear of being left alone

* Sudden clinginess

* Violent nightmares from which they wake screaming and crying

* Lashing out

* Angry, violent or antisocial behaviour.

Please note some of these behaviours are common in children generally, and one or two alone does not always indicate/suggest abuse. I hesitate to continue with this;

it's difficult without being there to evaluate the situation in person, so if you notice a few of these behaviours, be more watchful and have the 'inappropriate touching' talk.

Tell the child they should tell you immediately if this happens or if they feel uncomfortable around an adult or another child. Anyone at all, really. Make sure they know they should talk to you if they feel scared, confused, or threatened and you will protect them.

IMPORTANT INFORMATION: Sexual predators and abusers are not always or only men. Sometimes they are older/younger children; sometimes they are women or sometimes they are even brothers or sisters, fathers, mothers, aunties, uncles, cousins, friends, other family members, teachers, doctors and so on and so forth. There are different types of abuse, not just sexual. There is physical, mental/psychological, emotional (and probably spiritual abuse too) all with different ranges, from relatively mild to severe, and all forms of abuse can happen to anyone at any age and are unacceptable and deeply damaging.

Never post photos online of your kids naked or just in underwear. Be mindful of poses they are striking if just in swimwear, e.g. little girls with their legs spread or little boys bending over, that sort of thing. Don't share these sorts of pictures. Normal people just see a kid in swimmers, but predators would see that as provocative, arousing and alluring.

Always be watchful for anyone, even other children who stare or look at your kids a bit too long, or too often. Most predators generally lure their victims in by forming a relationship with them, and because children are so trusting and unaware, this makes them easier to trick and control. It's typically someone you already know. Within or close to the family.

If you suspect your child has been hurt or is being hurt, you need to find out who the perpetrator/s is/are right away and make sure the police are informed immediately. In case this is not blatantly obvious, do not allow that person/s near your child ever again, and do not allow your child to go anywhere alone until that person is in police custody. Get the child to repeat the details of the trauma at least twice in a row; record this if you can. Hold and comfort them while they do so or at least hold their hand (especially if it's not your child). Explain to them that it's not their fault, that some adults are bad people, but reinforce they are safe with you. It's very difficult to explain sexual abuse to children. Find a good counsellor specializing in sexual abuse.

When working with an abused child, I always start with 'Hi, I'm Izzy. I know someone hurt you, but you're safe with me. I'm a counsellor and I'm going to help you.'

If things get too intense and difficult, I find making a farting noise helps. I blow a raspberry on the inside of my bent elbow; it sounds like a huge fart. I then look at the child (as straight faced as I can manage) and say, 'Excuse me, I must have eaten something reeeally bad.' giggling will ensue. If it becomes too overwhelming for them to talk about, ask them other things like their favourite colour, ice cream flavour, music, sport, etc. to restore calm and control. Taking a break for a walk and/or ice cream or treat/reward is good too.

Some children will lash out with anger and violence. This is normal and understandable. Do not respond with discipline right away, talk to them about their overwhelming feelings. Get them to draw, distract them with friends and fun activities. If after eight-ish months they are still behaving with violence and anger, then talk to their counsellor about maybe employing some gentle discipline. Make sure you explain to the child as clearly as possible that what happened to them has made them angry and that's normal to feel that way, but it's not ok to behave that way. Ask them to tell you when they are feeling overwhelmed, or like they can't cope.

I worked with a little boy like this once; he was a good friend's son (and his father knew me well enough to trust my ground breaking new techniques), so when regular counsellors failed, he asked for my help. He said, 'I've tried everything. We can't get through to him. I don't see the sweet, loving little boy he used to be. We are losing him, Miss Kitten. Please help?'

Zac was so very angry, and he refused to talk to anyone about it or let anyone near him, so I suggested we talk to a teddy bear and pretend it was the person who hurt him. I joined in with him, beginning by asking the teddy bear why it thought it was ok to hurt someone else like it did.

Zac ended up screaming at the teddy bear and yelling, throwing things, and generally losing his head, so I went over (again, I do not suggest anyone copy my techniques, I am very good at what I do and able to read people and assess situations quickly, accurately and expertly) and I gently trapped his arms against his body. I picked him up and I held him gently but tight (more in a comforting way, only lightly restraining) Then I started singing. He became frightened and thrashed angrily for a while, so I gently patted his shoulder, telling him he was safe. Then he started to calm. I said, 'Sweetheart, I'm so sorry you were hurt, and you're allowed to be angry. It's not fair and shouldn't have happened. But you can't stay angry forever; that's not very fun.' I told him I was hurt too, and for a long time I was angry, and I asked him if he would like to talk to me secretly about what happened, since I understood.

We sat there with him crying in my arms for over an hour, talking about it over and over in detail until he felt better. Then I took him for a walk in the park and ice cream.

That evening, I lose my head pretty bad, triggered by Zac's horrible abuse story. I get drunk, walk 10 km to a theme park, climb a rollercoaster, get stuck and have to call Hol and Bunny to come and rescue me. Carrying the burdens of others becomes too hard and heavy for me sometimes.

The anger and violence disappeared from Zac's behaviour right away and I worked with him and his family, teaching them how to be more supportive and understanding; teaching him how to deal with his feelings and communicate when he was struggling. He is perfectly fine now. Zac was the first child I ever worked with and I already knew him, he trusted me, so it was easier. Seek professional help from someone who specializes in sexual abuse, there are some tough, uncomfortable, disturbing questions and feelings (pleasure & pain) related to this sort of abuse that need to be addressed right away.

I keep in touch with abused children, they need me again when they hit puberty and start thinking about normal sex stuff.

But this is also a good example of why appropriate affection is so important. Everyone gave that little boy space, and it was the wrong thing. Kids need to know they are still lovable after being violated in that way. Just as any adult would and does. Explain that what happened was wrong and shouldn't have happened to them, praise and reward them for being brave and telling the truth.

You need to work slowly at earning their trust. Obviously find professional counselling ASAP but honestly, in the direct aftermath, it's important to give the child safe, loving attention, concern and affection. If it isn't your child, the lines are blurry here, but still be attentive and kind, maybe just a hand on their upper back or shoulder in a comforting way.

Not all children will be comfortable with physical affection after being abused, so first ask them if it's ok if you touch or hug them; I usually say something along the lines of 'I know you have been through a hard and scary time and that someone has hurt you, but I'm a safe adult and I want to help you and make sure you're alright. Is it ok if I hold your hand or hug you? Are you comfortable with that?' It varies greatly with each child, most of them desperately need comforting and a hug, others are more reserved, so I start with holding their hand while they talk, but let them guide you.

But if the child becomes angry or frightened, let it go and be even more gentle, kind and understanding. Once I've earned their trust, I just ask if it's ok to hug them, hold their hand, or at least to put my hand on their shoulder (because I need to gauge their physiological response. I'm always upfront about my techniques). It's very important to talk to them a lot about what happened.

Not all children will welcome safe affection and that's normal; just gently work at earning their trust and don't push the affection thing, though it is essential.

> <u>Just an important note here</u>: most regular counsellors will tell you it's not appropriate to touch children right after they have been abused and that's partly correct, because in these circumstances, it can be confusing for a child. So be careful, communicate with the child and have a second adult present, especially in the beginning when you're getting to know the child (or the whole time if you feel it's required, but be aware this

will be more embarrassing, distressing and harder for the child).

I insist the parents attend the first two sessions during which I start with earning trust and getting to know the child - I do not talk about the abuse in front of the parents - unless the child specifically requests it - I don't recommend you ever do that. That's a whole different, far more complex and complicated situation. The whole family needs counselling and support then! It traumatises the parents too. (I might have to write a second book on this.)

Nevertheless, in my opinion, being appropriately affectionate is actually extremely important and I get the best results with that. I have noticed that children who are not given safe affection soon after abuse appear to end up with higher anxiety, low self-confidence and social problems. They also seem to feel like they are dirty or less; however, I have a relatively small test group. You do need to be VERY careful here, consult with a professional as needed. As always, communication is the key.

Also ask the child if they have any questions, or if there's anything they would like to talk about. Use the words 'Anything at all, it's just between you and me'. You will usually get some seriously weird and disturbing questions from kids who have been sexually abused. Good luck with that. Eeek.

The following goes for all forms of abuse: sexual, physical, mental, emotional, and psychological.

The first step you need to take: Obviously, you need to contact the police straightaway and remove the child/person from the dangerous situation IMMEDIATELY. <u>There is imminent potentially life-threatening danger</u> if an abuser suspects the child (particularly) or person is telling or seeking help. If it was me, I would physically remove the child/person from the situation quickly and take them straight to the police or keep them safe in my care. But this is not always possible, and I don't see too many people having the courage to do that. This is understandable. I have been there alone in a seemingly unending nightmare of being hurt, used and abused. I have worked on cases where the victim was murdered to silence them. So I know how critical it is to get someone (a child specifically) to safety immediately.

Step 2: Letting the person know they are safe with you and can tell you/talk to you about absolutely anything and you will protect them (especially if it's a child). When a child's trust has been broken, they are confused, angry and scared. Being a safe adult to them is something you have to work at slowly. Also let them know you are their friend and are always on their side and won't be angry at them. Children greatly fear getting in trouble for telling. This is more difficult as a parent. It's important to let the child or person know they are not alone and you can be trusted and want to help.

It's crucial to get them to repeat the details of the trauma two or three times in a row during the acute phase (as soon as possible after trauma). Try to put your hand on their shoulder or arm or hug them so you can gauge physiological response. Each time, look for stiffness and tension in muscles, breathing rate, pulse if you can and temperature of skin. Try to be aware if the skin turns clammy or sweaty. I know some of this is difficult without medical monitors, but I can do it. So just do your best to monitor it and see if it changes each time.

You know you have won when the person's voice is steady and their muscles and body relaxed, their skin cool and breathing unaccelerated.

The terrible, unfair, and disturbing truth is there are horrible side effects to all kinds of abuse, especially sexual abuse. Really horrifying things happen in the world everywhere and range from inappropriate touching, which is still abuse and deeply damaging to a child, to full blown vile, terrifyingly violent paedophile rings, like my experience. But the child who was inappropriately touched will be damaged and traumatised too.

It doesn't matter how bad it was or wasn't; it is still a violation of basic human rights and it's still abuse. So much harder for a child who has no ability to understand the adult things they are being subjected to. There is no instance whatsoever in which the child is at fault. Not ever. The good news is, you can heal yourself and live a happy life.

Side effects from trauma and overcoming them

Everyone reacts to traumatic experiences differently. Some people who have been sexually or physically/

psychologically/ emotionally abused might react differently and have different side effects to me, but in my experience, most people have the same or worse. This is consistently observed in all traumatic experiences, even bullying or just being left out. For example, one person might be so badly affected by being bullied they end their own life, while another just sinks into depression, isolation and self-harm, others are almost completely unaffected. It's all subjective and uniquely relative to each person's experiences and upbringing, largely influenced by their family life. Of course, nature plays a small part too. That, however, is a debate for another day.

Everyone is affected and responds completely differently. So I've come up with treatments and coping mechanisms that are applicable to most situations, problems and personalities.

Learning to objectively recognise, observe, and dissect behaviours and feelings is the first step to understanding, then controlling and ultimately overcoming bad/unwanted behaviours and feelings. Many psychiatrists and doctors will try to put you on medication.

Just FYI, it usually does more harm than good, (a lot of them cause brain damage, depression and suicidal urges, among other things.) Except in extreme situations where it is inarguably required. However it usually is just a temporary and somewhat inadequate band aid. You really need to work on the causal issues of your problems if you want to control and overcome anything.

Still, discuss this in depth with your doctor, but keep in mind, the doctor probably gets kickbacks from drug companies. Extreme cases include things like schizophrenia, violent behaviour and very severe depression and suicidal tendencies, etc. <u>Do not take this as medical advice; it is a warning.</u> Always listen to your doctor if you have extreme or severe symptoms. Getting a second opinion is a good idea but consider a naturopath or natural health expert for the second opinion. There are many herbs (St Johns wort is great) and natural remedies that are very effective, as well as things like acupuncture. Yep. I'm telling it how it is.

One of the biggest side effects from trauma is a fractured personality. This can be a secondary result of disassociation. Disassociation is when somebody experiences trauma, if they aren't helped properly and/or soon enough and are unable to process the situation, the pain and fear/confusion/traumatised feelings become too great; there is a part of them, or their personality, that disconnects or gets cut off in an attempt to kind of contain and isolate the pain.

I have seen this many times. In severe cases, a fractured personality becomes like a Dr Jekyll and Mr Hyde act, it is frequently misdiagnosed as multiple personality or bipolar disorders. Narcissistic behaviour is also usually born from this. This generally occurs when the person does not seek and/or has inadequate help, and/or a family member or partner fails to understand and be patient and caring. They feel completely isolated and alone. People lose touch with themselves as they try to deal and cope with the pain alone and often become hard, angry and push people away, distancing themselves from real life, often turning to drugs and/or alcohol.

This can be healed/ reversed with proper counselling and support, understanding and love.

A bit like my fireman, who had a fractured personality; he was the sweetest man at times but would turn into an angry, jaded, impenetrable jerk. I just shut out and pushed everyone away, but Holly fought for me, refused to give up, and eventually reached me.

Then this is followed by social isolation, withdrawal not only from life but also from most emotions. I find this is obvious in people's faces. If you care enough, you can see when someone's smile isn't real. You can see their personality change and then shrivel. You have to be gentle and understand this is a deer-in-headlights kind of scenario. Move slowly but show them you care and, above all, that they are safe. Work at proving you are trustworthy. The people who have been hurt the worst need the most work. You must bravely be committed to scaling the barbed wire reinforced walls of the lonely prison they built around themselves for protection, and prove over and over you're for real, you're trustworthy and you genuinely care.

If you're reading this and you were abused too, I know there are behaviours, not just sexual but also emotional, that are strange and beyond your control.

This is totally normal, and the worse the abuse, the stranger and more disturbing the behaviours. (E.g. self harm, irrational thoughts and behaviour, compulsive lying -this is actually a defence mechanism, compulsive eating, lashing out, agoraphobia, difficulty communicating, elective mutism, to name a few.)

Once you realise and accept this, you can overcome them all. When you were being hurt, you were not in control. You were forced to do things you didn't want to do, to feel things you didn't want and shouldn't have had to feel. But you're an adult and you're free. You are in control now. It takes a little bit of brain rewiring, but you can heal the damage, fix yourself and set yourself free.

There is no reason for you to hurt, blame or punish yourself, which is something I did most of my life. I promise you, it's normal. Completely. There's nothing wrong with you. You are not disgusting and certainly do not deserve to die or be hurt in anyway. It is disgusting and disturbing and horrible to go through these things, but it's not your fault nor in your control. Understand that; forgive and be understanding of yourself.

The thing about being groomed for sex abuse is it's a grooming that sticks with you for a lifetime. Twenty-ish years on, if someone initiated something sexual in a situation where I felt vulnerable or taken advantage of, I had no option, I just froze and had to submit. Even though I wanted to scream and punch and run, I froze up, a prisoner to the ingrained grooming. Then I had to allow and partake in sexual things even though I didn't want to do it. I shut off all my emotions and I tried to go as far away in my head as possible. Then I'd count, just like when I was little and all the other times through my life. But I realised after the last time, after the revolting massage rat, that I don't have to do this anymore. I'm an adult now, I'm in control, and I broke the grooming pattern, finally free! Hells yea baby!

Part of this had to do with the men I met and the changes they caused in my life: Dr Anthony and the son of Zeus, plus the fireman too. Being in the presence of men I knew would never hurt me helped. Search for someone who makes you feel totally safe and at ease.

I had a client, who is now a close friend, who was sexually abused by four male family members and she told me during one of our sessions, 'I liked it.' I explained all children like attention and affection, and she said, 'No, I actually thought it felt good to be touched like that.'(This is actually quite common, nothing to be ashamed about.)

I won't lie, it really threw me and I felt disgusted, angry and nauseated. It very nearly triggered me. I was silent for a good two minutes trying to process and understand and anchor myself to the present, but then I saw tears streaming down her face and her nails dug deep into her arm. As she was talking, I reached out and stopped her hurting herself, holding her hand and explaining that the human body can feel and respond to pleasure from a very young age. That's not something she can understand as a child and it's incredibly confusing.

However, it is still normal and something that sexual predators are usually aware of and exploit. Irrespective of whether she liked it or not, it wasn't something she wanted, asked for or invited in any way. It isn't her fault. She was the innocent child and victim.

I still believe she confused enjoying intimacy and attention with sexual pleasure or convinced herself she liked it in order to survive it. Regardless, I taught her how to love, understand and forgive herself. She now has a great husband and two young daughters. I worked with them as a family, and it was her brave idea to share this in here. It's not easy to undo the damage, but it is possible!

If you wake after nightmares of being abused and find yourself aroused, this is normal. Masturbating in your sleep is normal. I know it's horrible and gross, but it's a normal physiological response to sexual pleasure. Think about it: women get aroused thinking about their sexual experiences, and men have wet dreams. This is common, intrinsic human physiology. It is, for the most part not within our control; it's not your fault or any reflection on you at all if your first sexual experience is forced on you as an innocent child.

You are not at fault at all. Your body's responses are normal; again, rewiring your brain slowly in little positive ways is the answer. Change the way you think, just like I did. Also, find and focus on other sexual things that you find arousing.

On a personal note, unrelated to the text on sexual abuse above, the way I dealt with my trauma and the things lacking in my life was to be everything I needed. In my head when I was a child, I'd be my mother, and if I hurt myself, I'd be kind, attentive and concerned in my mind. Because no one was nice to me, I had to be nice to myself. I learnt how to counsel myself. As an adult, I kind of still do this and it allows me to distance myself and view many situations objectively, almost as a third party. Which actually gives me the psychological advantage. I have simply found my own way to exist and function in a world where I've experienced horrible things and everyone copes differently.

You have to find your own way to cope, and the way to quiet the turmoil within. The answer to that is firstly accepting yourself and being confident in yourself.

Let me tell you a secret: you are absolutely perfect just as you are. You're brilliant! The right people will see you, accept you and adore you. Those people who don't, that don't treat you as you deserve, tell them to bugger off. Walk away, you owe no one anything but yourself.

It's you and you; your opinion is the only one that matters. Other people's perceptions and judgements are skewed and influenced by their own lives, experiences and level of intelligence. The only competition is to better yourself, be better than you were yesterday, last week, last year.

Be your own best friend. If I can achieve this, anyone can. I had to rewrite my neural pathways in so many ways, to learn how to not hate myself. But it will be much easier for you, just keep working at it. You will win, and it will only take a month or two to see the improvement. Here are some ideas:

* Write down the things you like about yourself, and start journaling (recording and exploring your own feelings and emotions in detail.)

* Repeat self-love affirmations looking in the mirror, as I suggested previously.

* Take yourself out to your favourite activity or dinner, even if you go alone.

* Find hobbies and activities you enjoy.

* Tell yourself you're great just as you are and mean it because you seriously totally are. You rock, you can achieve and overcome anything!

* Reinvent yourself. Get a new hair colour/style, new outfit, take the course you always wanted, learn a language or skill.

Be brave and trust in yourself. You can do it; the power is within you. Remember, the ONLY opinion that matters is your own. You are the only person you need to impress. You don't need to do anything else; you don't need to impress people, only you. The right people will be impressed by and drawn to your strength and confidence. If people are mean, it's usually jealously. Just smile and keep walking, you're busy working on you. You don't have time for that BS.

The real perfection is imperfection and in embracing yourself exactly as you are. The most important and longest relationship you will ever have is the one with yourself. Make sure it's a loving happy relationship!

There are some of us who will end up in destructive and/or abusive relationships, and again this is normal too. I got sucked in myself, so desperate for a father I let an old man use me for sex. But I also had that extremely bizarre (honestly, that's the best adjective I've got for how weird the situation became) experience with the sleazy massage rat who was a narcissistic predator, and oh my gosh did I get very tangled, addicted and stuck in that web.

I wanted more because it held some reminiscence of the narcissistic predatory attention I got as a child, and that was the only even slightly affectionate touch and attention I received as a child. I.e. Because I associated predators and abuse with attention and affection, I will always be drawn to similar situations and people; perpetually searching for the love I desperately needed as a child. Unfortunately, I had to keep going back because his massage actually helped my muscles. It was the only thing that worked after the accident. Also just being near him fed the addiction. I was quite literally stuck between a rock and a seriously fucked up place. Please excuse my disgusting language there, it is required as an adjective, shall we say Poetic license?

It was so hard for me to break free because he was a predator and felt like a friend at first. It made it even harder for me to walk away.

I intensely despised him after the first two sessions because of the way he treated me. He was so mean to me, took advantage of me in so many ways. I still kept going back for more. He was like a bad drug and I wanted more, but also because I needed massage. He treated me so badly, and then blamed me. Similar to when I was little, I kept going back because those men were the closest thing I knew to family. They only wanted to hurt me and rape me, use me and beat me, but they wanted me around and I was so very desperate for that. These patterns will repeat again and again, until you recognize, address, actively control and heal them.

On another note, this was my first experience with a narcissistic personality as an adult, and you can't reason with them. No matter how logically, profoundly or rationally you explain or how much you try to dumb it down, they can't hear you because they believe they know everything and everyone. You just have to feel sorry for them, sigh and run away, which can be hard when you're under their spell, but you just gotta run. Narcissistic abuse has been shown to cause brain damage in victims.

Many women end up with men who beat them or hurt/torment them and again, it's a totally normal, abuse-related repercussion because it's what you know. Thankfully, I broke free from both men, and you can too! Look at the situation/relationship you're in, the person you're with, take a step back, and ask yourself if it's healthy?

Do you feel loved, respected, understood, safe and comfortable? If the answer is no it's time to make a change. And it's never too late. These are normal abuse-related behaviours and they can be overcome. The first step is being aware of the patterns, understanding the cause and realising you're in control and that you can change.

Ask friends to help separate you, and find somewhere with safe, understanding people.

This is very common in child abuse victims. But adapt ... If you constantly go for father/mother figures or abusive relationships: recognise it's not your fault but also step back and acknowledge the pattern and accept that:

1. You need to change because you deserve better, and

2. You are strong enough and want to change because this is your life, you're awesome, and you can overcome anything. Again, work on slight changes at first e.g. If it's mother/father figures you can't stay away from, go for slightly younger men or women and keep making yourself go slightly younger each relationship, but also find an older male/female who you trust to have a platonic relationship with, platonic means intimate and affectionate but <u>not sexual</u>, this will often fulfil your need for older attention and acceptance.

Attachment to predators and abusers is not uncommon, especially for children but also throughout all your life. Many women end up with abusive, mean husbands. This is likely because they formed an attachment to their first abusers and they subconsciously seek relationships that are similar. Many predators, especially sexual predators, intentionally trick their victims into forming an emotional attachment.

Narcissists are especially good at this. They almost cast a spell on you by pretending to be everything you need and want. This is how they attract/capture, addict, control and manipulate their victims.

Some victims actually believe they love their abuser and their abuser loves and cares about them. It has nothing to do with love or care though. For example, when I was little, those men acted like they cared about me because they knew I was alone and desperate for family; when I was a teenager, my boss acted like a father figure because he knew I needed a dad; the massage rat acted all friendly and fun because he knew I needed a male friend at the time.

None of them cared. They just acted like what I needed to capture my attention and trick me into believing I wanted and needed them in my life so they could use, abuse and take advantage of me.

It's genuinely really hard to spot this sometimes, as predators are by nature good actors. It's how they trick their victims, reel them in and keep them prisoner. This is the hardest thing to recognise, and then break, because the emotional attachment is real and just human nature. (And gets worse & stronger over time) Let me clarify here: It is not real in the sense that the victim and abuser have an emotional connection. It's real in the way that you have formed an emotional/psychological attachment to your abuser. This isn't your fault; these are normal human feelings. This is technically a form of trauma bonding. If you start to feel caring, affectionate feelings in an abusive relationship or situation create distance. As hard as it is, you have to realise it's not real. They don't care about you. To an abuser, you are a thing, a toy, something for them to manipulate and use, then ultimately destroy.

Creating distance is the first and hardest step. It is the most important step though, create distance and then review the situation once your feelings calm a bit. It can be hard to fight the overwhelming feelings, but once you get some distance, start to examine the situation objectively, ask yourself:

1. Is this a safe place for me? Am I being treated with respect, or am I being taken advantage of and used? You need to recognise that you are being manipulated and taken advantage of, tricked.

2. You need to recognise and address the fake emotional attachment you have to your abuser and remind and convince yourself it isn't real, and it's not. I promise you, as strong and real as it feels, once you create distance and stop seeing them, it will fade. I promise as much as it hurts, it will fade in time. Then you will see the truth. Use distraction techniques and find other pleasurable activities that are not associated with your abuser/abuse in any way.

There is the truly scary potential for some victims to genuinely believe their attachment and connection to their abuser is real and that their abuser loves and cares about them and they are in love with their abuser. Some victims end up marrying or spending their life with their abuser, forever trapped in the spell. I experienced this with my boss. I truly believed he loved and cared about me, and I almost got stuck in that relationship indefinitely. I recognised the danger and tried to leave, even tried to leave earth, but he refused to let go and the more time I spent with him, the worse it got; the harder the spell was to break. I actually started thinking about spending my life with him, as a teenager with a man over 30 years my senior. Yuck. This is an example of how real and strong the bond and connection can feel. I was imprisoned. You CAN break free, Recognition, DISTANCE, distraction, and determination are essential.

Quite honestly, I am drawing a blank here. Each individual situation can vary so greatly, I can't possibly cover it all. My best advice is go on a holiday if you can. Get away, regain some control, ask friends to help separate you, cut them out of your life completely, or if you can't, see that person as little as possible.

I was going to write about overcoming generational trauma and breaking the cycle of abuse but have decided against that because I need to work with people in person so I can evaluate and make sure others are safe and you do not pose a threat to the safety of others.

I will say this however: awareness of certain behaviours and their triggers can help you modify any unwanted behaviour. For example, if your spouse looking at another man or woman triggers you and makes you angry, causing a fight in which you lose control, become very angry, mean, or violent. You must first recognise the trigger, reason with yourself and say to yourself, Right, ok, this is triggering unwanted emotions and behaviour, but they married me. It's normal human behaviour to look at attractive people. They are still with me; they love me. In a 'no harm, no foul' kind of attitude. Reason with yourself.

If you still feel yourself getting angry, upset, and losing control, excuse yourself from the situation, create distance, go for a walk, and calm yourself. Repeat the mantra below over and over in your head while taking long, deep breaths.

This is similar to how I work with people one-on-one, except, after talking to them, explaining and educating them, I go with them and deliberately expose them to their triggers so I'm there with them as they learn to recognise, observe and understand the causal issues and origins of these feelings. Then I help them tackle their emotional, physiological, and psychological reactions one at a time until they are in complete control: this is a big part of how I cure PTSD and other trauma and stress related problems and disorders, WITHOUT MEDICATION!! **DO NOT** under any circumstances attempt to do this without professional guidance and supervision. If you do it incorrectly, you could seriously mess yourself up and make things worse.

* Step 1: Recognise the trigger/s.

* Step 2: Recognise the unwanted behaviour the trigger/s cause.

* Step 3: Actively take control and refuse to let those behaviours take hold.

Repeat this:

I am in control.

* I am a good person.

* I am in charge of my own feelings and behaviour, and I recognise I've been triggered. I know what unwanted behaviours this causes in me and I will not lose control.

* I am strong. I am brave and in charge!

* I can rise above this. It's my behaviour; I can control it!

* I can and will overcome this. I am proud of myself.

If you cannot calm yourself and there is a danger of violence or uncontrollable behaviour, remove yourself from the situation immediately to ensure the safety of others and call a friend or family member for help, or an ambulance/the police. If you cannot trust yourself not to hurt or endanger others, call for an ambulance/the police immediately and run as far away as you can. Count back from 100 over and over until help arrives. Sing your favourite song loud and out loud. Calm yourself, focus hard on deep breathing. Never allow yourself to hurt others.

However, the first step is in recognising the triggers, being aware of the unwanted behaviours they cause and refusing to let them control you. Walk, run, eat, distract yourself, but do not under any circumstances turn to drugs or alcohol. This endangers not only everyone else but also yourself. You cannot control or overcome anything if you are under the influence. Don't do that to yourself babe. You can overcome this and be better. But once you move through your triggers and actively take control, it gets easier every time. Just keep going until you win.

This is how I overcame my own problems. I learned to recognise the situations that triggered me, which for me was people treating me badly and taking advantage of me, or someone being sexual and inappropriate towards me in an unwanted way. This would then trigger/cause unwanted behaviours in me, like drinking and hurting myself, forcing myself to sleep with a man and occasionally getting very angry at or yelling at strangers, predominantly strange men when they touched me. (Punched a few too, oopsy. Although, that was more in self-defence.) Self-defence or protecting others is the only acceptable form of violence.

Once I recognised the triggers and subsequent behaviours they caused in me (cause and effect), I was very aware, vigilant and when triggered, I kept control and I'd walk away and go for a walk or long bike ride to distract myself that way. It's fairly easy to control and move through once you recognise and are aware of the process.

You need to be supervised by a professional and have a back-up plan in place in case you have trouble, or it doesn't work. Then seek immediate assistance, call an ambulance or police if you believe you may be a threat to the safety of others or yourself.

With depression, suicidal thoughts and anxiety, sometimes you need to talk to yourself in your head and just remind yourself you need to be strong, keep control and push through; you will come out the other side. Once you push through, reward yourself with praise and a treat of some sort. It will get easier every time.

The most pertinent advice I can give you is that loving, caring about, listening to, and being there for people and being acknowledged, accepted and included are all most people need, yourself included and foremost. This is how we change and reunite the world in a #RETURN TO LOVE. Relearn to love, accept and cherish yourself, then everyone else.

Tips from Jasper:

Things my friend, Kitten taught me about being a great man:

- *   It's not sex; it's making love. Be discerning of who you share your body and time with.

- *   Always be a chivalrous gentleman.

- *   Always open doors for women.

- *   If on a date, kiss her on the cheek, compliment her and tell her she looks beautiful when you pick her up, always walk her right to her door after.

- If you're not early, you're late.

- Never swear or use foul language.

- Never, ever raise your voice to or get angry with a woman. If she's upset you, calmly discuss it, like a mature adult.

- Listen, truly listen and see her.

- Always stick up for her.

- Violence should only be used to protect yourself and others and always a last resort.

- Always be open and honest especially about your feelings.

- Behave with honour and integrity constantly.

- If someone tests you or behaves badly, always be the bigger man: ask if they are ok, talk to and try to help them; if this fails, walk away.

- Be brave and always be the first to step forward to help.

- If a girl cries, hug her, tell her she's safe with you, and talk to her. Show genuine, caring affection. Try to help with whatever she is upset about.

- Communication is paramount in all situations.

- Help everyone and be kind wherever you can.

* Be mature and act with thoughtful maturity in difficult situations. Take a moment to think, what's the best way to handle this problem?

* Always dress nicely and speak properly and politely.

* Strive to make the world a better place, and lead by being an awesome example and role model for others.

* If you feel yourself getting angry, walk away.

* Always protect and stand up for/by your friends and everyone.

* Treat everyone with respect and kindness, irrespective of their behaviour.

* Walking away from a fight makes you more man than coward.

* Women need to be seen, heard, loved, understood and protected first and foremost. They need to feel safe and comfortable, appreciated. Much more then they need bracelets or flowers, though those are good too.

* Always stand up for what's right, regardless of everyone else, even if you stand alone.

* Being openly affectionate and honest about your feelings is important.

* It's ok, actually, it's good for boys and grown men to cry and show open emotions/ be emotional. Men hurt and need/deserve to be comforted and cared about just as much as women. They also need to know they matter and are loved and appreciated. Be supportive too. It's good to hug other men when they cry, are upset or need support.

We are taught no one is perfect. That's wrong. We should be taught EVERYONE is perfect. It is so important to always be yourself completely and confidently, and also to be open, honest, caring and loving with everyone. Always tell those close to you how you feel and how much they matter. Life is so fragile, and you truly never know when the last time you will see, speak to or touch someone will be. Make every single second count.

Your friend, Kitten's important life lessons:

- ♥ Life is short, so be yourself completely. Do what you love and enjoy everything regardless of the opinions of others. The truth is people will always judge and talk anyway, so just be yourself and enjoy your life, ignore the haters.

- ♥ ALWAYS BE GRATEFUL FOR EVERYTHING you have: Life, health, peace, safety, food, shelter, family, friends etc.

- ♥ Love hard.

- ♥ Forgive quickly.

- ♥ Other people's behaviour has little to do with you personally and more to do with the secret battles they fight within. Understanding this makes everything easier. It's not you; it's them.

- ♥ Strive to be the best version of yourself and help/inspire and encourage others do the same.

- ♥ Accept everyone as they are.

- ♥ Life is a constant work of art and you can start over any time and as many times as needed.

- ♥ The best place to find yourself is alone in nature.

- ♥ *EVERYONE* DESERVES TO BE LOVED.

- ♥ Be kind to and gentle with yourself and everyone else.

- ♥ <u>Always stand up for and fight for what's right.</u>

- ♥ Be kind to and help everyone every chance you get.

- ♥ LOVE IS ALWAYS THE ANSWER.

- ♥ Some people won't apologise because they can't.

- ♥ Walk away from disrespect.

- Reasonable, calm, logical arguments are not always enough, sometimes, you have to go in with guns blazing.

- Learn self-defence. Never start a fight, but always be ready to protect yourself and others if needed.

- Real maturity and the ability to understand think and communicate like an actual adult is rare but underrated. It is something I am trying to teach, inspire and recultivate.

- <u>Always stick together in the face of adversity. There is safety (& power) in numbers.</u>

- Always lead by example.

- Pick up litter.

- Adopt homeless animals (and people).

- Every single person, plant and animal is a living being and has a right to life, even ants, spiders, bugs, cockroaches and animals we consider pests. Studies show they communicate, have familial bonds, and feel pain and emotions just like us. Plants and trees too, they communicate with each other. They have just as much right to life as us. Ending lives at random is not ok. Everything has a soul.

- You never know how long you have with someone and when your last moment will be, so you have to always be open and honest and tell people how you feel. Lives can change and end in milliseconds. I lost someone in less than twenty minutes once. I've lost people I never even realised I was in danger of losing. Always say, 'I love you,' and try not to end in anger or disagreement. Let them know how great they are and how much they matter, not just to you but in general. People need to be reassured of their importance and place in the world.

♥ Other people's behaviour is a reflection on them and how they feel inside, not you. Don't take it personally. The majority of the time, it has nothing to do with you at all!

♥ Some people will take advantage of, betray and let you down. Never respond with anything other than kindness and grace. Forgive and be understanding, but don't allow it to happen more than once. You have every right to walk away from toxic people, protect yourself and your energy.

♥ Always be kind and respectful to everyone. You never can tell who is teetering on the edge of a ledge. Your act of kindness may save a life.

♥ Understand not everything is always as it seems, in black and white. Always trust your instincts.

- ♥ You can't always help everyone or win ... sometimes you just have to let go, walk away. But never underestimate the value of planting a seed.

- ♥ Be careful who you allow into your life, not everyone has good intentions. Sometimes the most dodgy, unscrupulous people are the best actors.

- ♥ Help everyone where you can, but remember you are the most important. Always choose you first.

- ♥ Not everyone will be able to hear you or see you; this means they aren't meant for you. The people and relationships meant for you will come with ease and safety. Never chase or beg.

- ♥ Conduct yourself in a polite manner and behave with honour and integrity always. Irrespective and regardless of what others are doing, you are only responsible for, and in control of, your own behaviour. Set a good example.

- ♥ Similarly, always fight for and stand up for what's right and just, regardless of the crowd.

- ♥ Help and protect those who need it. Stand up for everyone, plants/nature, trees and animals especially - they have no voice with which to protest, communicate, beg for mercy, nor cry or scream in pain.

- ♥ Don't believe everything you see and hear (in the media/news especially) There is misleading information and subliminal messaging and programming everywhere. Open your eyes listen and think. Educate yourself.

- ♥ 'No' is a complete sentence and requires no further explanation or information.

- ♥ Compliment others. Make them smile and feel happy. 'You look gorgeous in that colour' is an easy one, and everyone loves to hear it.

- ♥ Always be yourself in every way. You are unique and so perfect. If you don't feel comfortable and safe to do so, you need to find new people who give you the freedom and space to honestly and completely be yourself. Shine Baby!! Also learn to have fun alone and enjoy your own company.

- ♥ Believe in and be true to yourself. You have to be your own best friend and biggest fan. You are incredible.

- ♥ Understand that every single person is doing their absolute best and operating at the highest level that their intelligence, perceptions and life experiences allow. Love everyone exactly as they are. Encourage them. Help them grow.

- ♥ Trust in God's plan. Sometimes you need to have faith and just do your best every day.

- ♥ The only real failure is not trying. You will have good days and bad days, and that's normal. Sometimes the best plan of action is to set everything aside and rest and recharge, for as long as you need. Then come back to it when you're good, and you will come good, as long as you fully allow yourself to rest. There is a big difference between exhaustion and laziness; don't confuse the two. Don't be hard on or beat yourself up. Just rest, watch funny movies.

- ♥ Always give everything your best shot, your all. At the end of the day, you will regret the things you didn't do and the opportunities you missed much more than the mistakes you made.

- ♥ Try and cultivate the ability to see the best in every situation and be thrilled with tiny bits of progress. Recognise the hope and potential all around you.

- ♥ Follow in my paw steps, be brave and be a light in the darkness. Help me change the world!

When overcoming trauma by yourself and looking within, try this: Start a journal: Write down every detail of the trauma at least three times. Write down any emotions this brings up, and be aware of anything at all related to the trauma that triggers anxiety, depression, etc. Come up with a plan to face triggers and be aware and mindful of behaviours this causes.

Allow yourself to fully feel all emotions associated with the trauma. I'm going to use the example of a romantic relationship breakup here: write about your relationship, both the good and the bad and how you felt in the relationship and about that person. Say, for example, things that trigger sadness and depression in you are looking at things they gave you or hearing songs that remind you of them, etc. Write it all down. Write how you feel without them and allow yourself to feel it, really feel the emotions and understand them. Write everything down, say the things you need to say, and if you have unresolved feelings or questions, write them a letter/text/email... send it or don't, it doesn't matter, just get it out. Burn it after, focus on releasing everything.

After you've given yourself sufficient time to really look at everything and deeply feel it all, you will start to feel inner peace and resolution. Then make the decision to let them go and move on. Then do so, use distraction techniques if needed. Have fun, the solution is working through it all. This can be applied to most traumatic experiences. However, if you experience severe emotions or reactions to triggers, make sure you have a friend, family member, or professional close by who can watch over you and make sure you're ok. Most bad feelings pass if you can push through or distract yourself. If in doubt, or if you have concerns, seek out a professional.

Ok guys, this has been a very draining, difficult time for me, and I'm officially signing off to go live my life. I have one request though: please help me continue my pay-it-forward and #RETURN TO LOVE and community movement worldwide. Do something nice. Buy a homeless person a meal and winter coat/blanket, adopt a stray animal, help a friend in need, and give someone who needs it money, or pay for their groceries. Be there for someone in need; it doesn't even have to be big, but done with kindness, love and good intention. Instead of paying you back tell them to do the same, pass it on. I am trying to turn the world around and reunite everyone through love and community. My final message is a reminder to everyone: there is strength, power and safety in numbers and that's literally all it's going to take to turn the world back to right. No matter how scary and how far gone, at the end of the day, if enough of us stand up & say no, they lose, end of story. Social conditioning has been separating us for decades on purpose, but it's time to reunite. To stand together in love, unity, strength and friendship. We are all family, after all.

Help me change and reunite the world so we can fight for freedom and right together. #ReturnToLove. One for all, all for one!

Peace baby,
Your friend, *Kitten*.

The Ending

One day Kit and I came home to find a tiny bird trapped inside the foyer of our apartment building. It was terrified, repeatedly smashing itself into the glass walls desperately trying to get out, Kit talked to it, trying to calm it, telling it: "everything will be ok sweetheart we will help you." We stood there with the door open trying to help it; it just frantically smashed itself, flying into the glass walls as hard as it could. Kit pleaded: "darling please stop, you're going to hurt yourself." Eventually the little bird became unsteady on its feet. It was really getting to Kit, she begged it to stop. Her voice laden with torment and anguish. It smashed itself into the glass and fell to the ground unable to get up. Kitten rushed over and softly spoke to it, then she gently picked it up, very softly stroked its back and started singing. Daryl Braithwaite 'the horses'. She looked at me with tear filled eyes, "its little hearts beating so hard, we have to go to the vet!!"

There was a look on her face that held a new, different, deeper kind of pain. Worried that taking it with us would only stress it further, we walked to the garden and she gently put it in the grass while we went to get a box, she told it not to worry, everything would be ok and we'd be back soon. On the walk upstairs she is really worried it might die alone. There was an odd pitch to her voice I'd never heard before, and she is shaking. We found a box, a little bowl and some water and hurried back downstairs. When we got there the little bird had flown away, apparently having recovered from the shock. I beamed at Kitten, she loved every little victory, of helping or saving someone. She lived for these moments that made her endless, unrelenting suffering worth it. But she wasn't smiling back at me like usual, she stuttered with a shaking voice: "that poor little birdy." Over and over, I replied that the bird was fine, it had flown away and she'd saved it. She just kept saying it repeatedly. I pointed to the bird as it flew to its family. "Look its fine, it's happy." I put my hand in her paw and I squeezed it, saying in a fifties style buoyant American news readers tone: " SuperKitten strikes again; saving yet another life." She takes a deep breath saying "that poor little birdy" I look at her face, she is crying. CRYING.

I'd never seen the tears actually fall and once she started, the dam burst and she crumpled to the ground and cries so hard still saying "that poor little birdy." Right then I realised how extremely sensitive she is and the level of pain she felt; not just her own, but everyone else's and how deeply she felt it. I also recognised that inside she felt like that little bird did, desperately trying to escape. I had an epiphany. I knew I had to let her go, I saw my own selfishness. I sit down and cuddle her, and I whisper in her ear: "I understand now baby, I truly comprehend how badly you hurt. I want you to know that if you need to go, you have my blessing." I cry too, apologising for being so selfish. I say "if you want to go, I understand that, I will let you go and I will keep your movements alive. I'm so sorry for trying to make you stay, for letting you suffer."

Kitten:

There was a little girl being horrifically hurt, and I promised her one day I'd take her away so no one could hurt her ever again. I failed to do this sooner, and she got hurt so much more. I fought to heal her and succeeded, but now I feel the call; it's time to set her free. All she ever wanted was to be loved, liked, accepted and appreciated. I couldn't protect her properly, but now she's had a chance to feel real happiness, and I'm so very proud of the young woman she grew into regardless of everything.

I'm so proud of her for surviving it all, but I'm letting her go, stepping away and moving into my adult life. I'm determined to learn how to love and to feel, to let people in and not be alone always. I'm determined to keep getting better and continue working towards changing/saving & reuniting the world.

I'm lying in bed half asleep next to Holly one night, and I can hear sirens, which isn't unusual for Chevron Island, but suddenly I realise I can smell smoke. I look out the window and see an orange glow and flames. I jump up instantly, grabbing the nearest clothes and shoes. I'm out the door in like a minute. Holly and I like to run together often. I'm up the street in less than 2 minutes after I woke up. I'm surveying the scene as I run, mapping out the house in my mind in case I need to help. There are eight firemen. I recognise the owner standing next to a fireman on the curb, so I run up to them. Holly is right behind me. The lady is telling him her young daughter is in an upstairs bedroom. He says it's too late, It's unsafe, and she's likely dead already. I think: are you freaking kidding me?!!???! I yell at him but I'm looking at the house, already planning the fastest and safest route upstairs.

She pleads; again he refuses, and I take off instantly, only seconds having passed since I arrived, sprinting towards the front door. A few of the firemen try to grab me, but I side-step them and tell them to back off. Adrenaline is pumping through my body. I know I'm going to get hurt bad this time and I decide that's alright, as long as I at least try to save the kid. I barely slow through the front door and have to kind of jump side to side to dodge the flames. I don't pause or think; I just run right into the little girl's room. My arms are on fire, so I grab a blanket off her bed and put them out (only because I can't pick her up if they are on fire; she might get hurt). It freaking hurts so bad, but I don't care! The little girl is crying. I tell her it's ok, I will save her.

There's a cat on her bed, so I tell her I'm going to pick her up but I need her to carry her cat in her arms really, really tight. She understands, so I grab her and she grabs the cat and a teddy bear. I tell her to put the blanket over her and the cat, then hold her breath. Once she's covered, I run back out and down, squinting against the heat, smoke and shattering glass that's flying everywhere. I know there are only mere milliseconds left before the house collapses.

I can't breathe, I'm dizzy AF, but I feel the girl shaking in my arms and feel a little furry tail brushing my elbow and hear a soft meow. I remember I'm carrying precious cargo and I dig deep, push forward, kick what's left of the flaming front door open and burst outside. The house collapses instantaneously behind me. My lungs are on fire, really hurting. I pull the blanket off so they can breathe. Fire, ambos and Holly run at us, I'm so happy the kid's safe. I've never smiled so big in my life. I'm feeling wicked bad dizzy. I didn't realise I'd been holding my breath almost the whole time. I cough out thick black smoke and blood - it hurts. Holly is saying something, but I can't really focus.

Jake, one of the ambos I see heaps comes over, shaking his head at me and smiling, about to tease me affectionately. Then he realises something is seriously wrong and his smile fades. I feel funny, kind of light-headed and like my head is going to explode from pressure at the same time. I fall down on my knees; then I start to lose consciousness. Its ok, I tell myself in my head. I saved the kid, a cat and a teddy bear (bonus). I did good. My lungs, chest and arms really really hurt and once again, I soothe myself through immense pain, fear, distress and trauma.

I tell myself, it's ok. I'm alright, I will be dead in a minute and it will stop hurting. Then I count. Just like I did when I was a little girl. For once though, I'm right ... finally I'm right, it will never hurt again. I actually thought I'd just pass out and wake up in hospital, but this time, it seems I'm actually leaving. They put me on a stretcher and the last thing I see is the little girl in her mum's arms, holding her kitty. They are smiling at me.

Fear and despair flood me as everything goes black. Sadly, finally when I want to live, when I want to try to learn to love, is when God decides to take me home. I'm so grateful for the experiences I got and the people I met. As I fade, I'm thinking …

No more firemen, friends, smiles. No Bunny, no Holly. No more licking chocolate off naked women. OMIGOSH no more big tits!!! My heart breaks. No, stop! I want to go back! I want to keep trying; I want to stay.

No more anything. As I start to slip away I can hear Holly's voice in my head, making a joke about God having to listen to the angels screaming my name in pleasure for eternity and I smile as tears slip from eyes (yes, this time I'm actually crying) and everything fades.

Weirdly, the last thing I remember is having a kitty purring and rubbing my face. I'm not entirely sure I didn't hallucinate that although, let's be realistic here. If I was hallucinating anything, it would be a different type of pussy on my face as I died. Excuse the crude double entendre, hehe, naughty Kitten.

There's a bright light and I can see my nanna and my friends I lost along the way. My grandfather whom I never met, my mum's brother and my pets. I see sunshine and I feel light and free and happy.

Finally free, finally home, forever. I watch my imprint and paw prints live on. I guess I did matter, after all. I watch Holly meet a woman, get married, and have a baby girl who she names after me. Not Bella, no, she calls her Kitten. Hehe. That poor kid.

I know you probably think this isn't a happy ending, but it is. I got what I always wanted: to grow up, change the world and then leave it. I have always done the right thing for everyone over and over, even if they treat me badly or take advantage. I gave them chances and I keep doing this. For reasons I never understood, no one ever returned the gesture.

On our honeymoon Holly said to me with tear filled eyes, 'Kitten, you are far too good for this world and some of the people in it.' I know somewhere deep inside, she could feel that time was running out, that I was leaving. She was right, but I don't mind. I made a difference; that's all that matters. Plus I got to feel free, feel happiness and enjoy sex, which was a big surprise. I got close to my mum and I got to have a dad. I fought and I tried so hard, and I won. I succeeded in changing the world and I healed myself. I was a huge success.

The second I get to Heaven, God grins at me, saying, 'hello, my little wild thing,' then looks over at all the gorgeous naked angels and sighs heavily. 'Well, where are my noise-cancelling headphones?' We laugh; he tells me how proud of me he is and how great I was. After long happy lives, Holly, Amy, my bro D and my mum and dad (Dr Anthony) join me, followed by everyone else I was close to.

I'm still up here making all the angels, strippers and girls scream with pleasure. Why do you think it rains so hard sometimes? Yep. That's my bad, not even a little bit sorry.

My soulmate is here too, we have four children, Matt, Raphael, Estella and Graciella and are so happy.

Amy

When my phone rings at some stupid hour, I answer without even looking at the screen. It's Holly, she is frantic. I can't understand a single fucking word she's saying other than 'Kitten'.

She's bawling so hard, I can't make any sense of what she's trying to say. I try to calm her, but she can't even hear me. A dark, heavy weight comes over me and my heart fills with desperate sorrow, this is the call I've always dreaded. I reach out through time and space with my soul, looking for my Kitten, but she's gone. There's no response, no connection. I want to scream and cry I want to drink; I want to die, I somehow manage to stagger to my neighbour and friend's house and ask her to drive me somewhere. I'm wearing the oldest, ugliest dress I own but I don't notice, I get to Holly's and practically fall out of the car. I stumble in and her face is red from crying, her features screwed up in pain. I feel like nothing is going to be good or fun ever again.

We sink to the floor and just lie there in a snotty pile, crying in the entry way. At some point, Zoe joins us. I fall asleep from exhaustion and wake up when Zoe and Holly get up. We go to the living room and talk about a funeral. We will have to hire the fucking football stadium. Holly says we should go to Kit's place and get all her pictures and stuff. So we drive over to Kitten's. We walk in and start crying again. There are pictures of us everywhere. There's a pile of photo albums on the bed with three letters on it for Hol, Bunny and her mum, plus a USB with this novel on it. She knew, somehow she knew, the end was near. We all cherished her - I hope she could see that.

We have the wake at my place. We make it the ultimate tribute to her. We start seriously and solemnly with close friends, celebrating her life and mourning her loss; then later we have a gigantic party with strippers. Yes, of course they have huge tits and we do body shots. Most of the strippers knew Kitten and they join in crying. We sit around talking about all the fun we had, all the adventures and all the craziness. We pass around photos and tell stories.

We play Kitten's songs: The Pussycat Dolls 'Don't Cha' (wish your girlfriend was a hot freak like her?), JT's 'Sexy Back' and of course, Ginuwine's 'Pony' and Ludacris 'What's your fantasy'. But we also play Zed 'Renegade Fighter', Katy Perry's 'Roar', Coldplay's 'Yellow' and 'The Scientist' and David Guetta's 'Titanium'.

Jack walks up with his daughters, and he drops to his knees, puts his hands on the urn and says, 'Bye Mum.

Thanks for saving me, for loving me and teaching me to love myself.' He has tears pouring down his face, and his two tiny twin daughters come to his side and say in little girly, childish voices, 'Bye bye Aunty Kitten. We love you and miss you so much forever,' then join their dad crying. I meet Holly's tear filled eyes, and all of a sudden it's too much, too unfair and I want it to be a bad dream.

I get up, run outside, drop to my knees and start screaming. Holly comes out and screams with me. I have never cried so much in my life. We are joined by our close friends. We all scream and cry. But when we couldn't scream anymore, Hol looks at me and says, 'at least she isn't hurting anymore Bunny. She's free, finally at peace.' I nodded numbly. But she is right.

One of the strippers comes out to tell us it was time to get ready for the big party. It is fantastically epic. All of my neighbours join in and the whole entire street is Bella's goodbye party. So many people come; it is massive. Police and ambulance turn up to say goodbye. Random people I'd never even seen before.

We have a few more strippers and we get lap dances (because we know she's watching from Heaven, teehee). All of her male model friends come and join in. I search every face for her fireman and the son of Zeus. I don't know if they came or even knew, but they made Kitten change. We love them for that.

It's a wild night, a truly well-deserved send off. A couple of thousand people come at least. We party until the sun comes up. We do a huge goodbye cheers to her at dawn. At the end, the little girl's mother and father walk up to us with tear-stained faces, say they are sorry but so grateful. I want to yell at and get angry at them, but I know that Kitten would have been really happy with the way things ended. She died a superhero. Even though she was a hero to so many every single fucking day, this was the perfect way for her to go: rescuing someone else. She saves eight more lives with her organ donation too.

Holly

One night we are lying in bed sleeping and Kit suddenly jumps out, grabs a crop top and shorts, throws them on and pulls on some sneakers. She grabs her phone and as she's running out the door, she's yelling that there's a fire. I get up quickly, look out the window: a house up the street is on fire. I can already see two fire trucks. I'm only moments behind her as she arrives at the scene. There's huge flames and thick black smoke. A woman is desperately explaining and pleading; her 5yr old daughter is in there, in her upstairs bedroom. The fireman is saying it's too late, there's no hope. My heart starts to pound.

Kitten yells at him in utter disbelief, 'There's a child in there!' I know exactly what's coming, out of the corner of my eye I can see her muscles twitching. I don't even bother to try to stop her, I see her slightly shift her stance and immediately she's gone. Three different firemen try to grab her as she flies towards the inferno, but she dodges them effortlessly, yelling 'Back off!' She pushes open the front door without pause and she's gone, disappearing into the flames and smoke.

I really should have taken her suggestion of tying her to the bed more seriously. I smile for a brief instant at that amusing and sexy idea.

I didn't know it then, but it is the last time I smile for a very long time. The fireman is asking her name, and I absently reply 'Kitten' wondering if I should go in after her. Suddenly anger overtakes me and I turn on him, on all of them, yelling 'Why aren't you doing your job? Go after her. It should be you in there, not her!'

They all refuse saying it's not safe. I'm watching the flames engulf the house rapidly, a thick plume of black smoke at least 30 feet in the air. My heart growing heavy and more desperate with every passing second, the moments passing with excruciating slowness. I'm seriously thinking of going after her, but I know there's no point. My heart breaks as the house begins to collapse in on itself with loud bangs of wood splintering under the heat and pressure and glass shattering and exploding. Nothing could possibly be alive in there. I bite my lip and begin to cry, thinking no Kitten, no. Please don't be gone baby gurl, Please.

Suddenly the front door kind of explodes open and rocKIT runs out with a little girl in her arms, clutching a teddy bear and a cat. Kitten saving a kitty. Touché. The firemen run forward to take the kid and cat from her arms, and ambulance officers rush forward to help the child. I run towards Kitten.

The mother bounds joyously to her daughter. As I get close to Kitten, I see she has really bad burns on her arms, her skin and muscle burnt away so bad you can see charred bone. But otherwise she looks like she is ok; she is beaming. I loved seeing her smile so hard, she is emanating pride. I am too, her quick thinking saved a child and an animal from absolute imminent death. There is not a single other person on this planet capable of that level of bravery and selflessness.

I start to her tell her I'm so proud but she doesn't say anything. I realise she looks strange, her eyes are all bulgy and her face is bright red. I yell for an ambulance officer. Jake, a guy we see often runs over. She kind of reaches out and touches me, then coughs out a huge cloud of black smoke and some blood. Jake says incredulously, 'Kitten, are you ok?' she responds by falling to her knees, then forward onto her face.

Like in a splatt, arms out wide, almost like she'd taken a running jump and belly flopped/ face planted herself on the ground. Always eccentric is my baby gurl, even in her last moments. Had to go out with a bang! They pick her up and put her on a stretcher. I grab the lady's cat and put it on Kit's belly. She always really loved animals, I guess because they never hurt her.

I know she's about to die, I can feel it: a deep, insurmountable sadness in my heart and soul. I put my hand in her paw, lean in and whisper, 'I love you, I'll see you on da flip side.' The cat rubs itself all over her face, purring. I feel it inside, the very second she dies, like a massive hole has been ripped inside me and I feel her paw turn limp as the life leaves her body. I look at Jake and I stutter, 'She's gone.' I look at the burns on her arms and I think with relief, that's the last time she will ever feel pain. He confirms it, his voice shaking and tears falling. She's left us.

I give the cat back, and the mother hugs her, crying too; then she goes over to Kitten's lifeless body, kisses her cheek, and says thank you. She's very upset she didn't get to say it before Kit died, but I tell her it's ok, that Kitten never needed any thanks for being a hero. It was the very essence of who she was, my Angel had superhero blood running through her veins. Then I collapse in grief. Kitten is gone; my love is dead. The cat and little girl are safe and well.

Kitten finally finds her peace.

The sun doesn't shine as brightly. Nothing will ever be fun ever again.

I can barely breathe, and most of the world will never even realise what it's missing.

But those who knew her know and they feel the gaping, barren, unfillable hole where Kitten should be. They noticed the whole world dim and turn a little bit colder; they feel the loss and pain. I know she would want us all to continue her mission of reuniting and changing the world, one person at a time, with love and kindness. So I tell everyone to do this, as she did, and we can make the world that Kitten was reaching for real. Y'all should help us too. Imagine how great the world would be if we do, say and act like she did. #ReturnToLove

Kitten was a gift to this world and she touched, loved and healed every single person she ever met. She really did change the world, and her love and special light will shine on through the lives of those lucky enough to have met her.

Just like that, everything's over, but she left us one last gift: this novel. I'm doing my best to finish this the way she would have wanted. Amy and I wrote her part of the ending. Dedicated to and in loving, heartbroken memory of KITTEN.

RIP Isabella (Kitten) Hansen, 1995–2022. The woman, the wonder, the miracle.

Kitten lived her life with the sole purpose of helping/healing/inspiring others and making the world a better place. She struggled through the pain of each day to achieve this. She set a fabulous example for the rest of us. RIP sweet little Angel.

I think now it's ok to cry for her. She is finally free. Finally safe.

Rest in peace my sweet RocKIT. Your love will echo through the ages.

The light and love you brought to this world will never ever fade. I love you baby gurl, higher than the sky, deeper than the ocean. You have left your sweet little paw prints over so many hearts.

I guess I knew this day would come, even though I hoped I was wrong and even through the sadness, I feel the relief. She isn't suffering anymore. All she wanted was to be liked, loved and accepted and she was, but she wouldn't let herself see it. We all adored you Kitten. May you finally feel whole and be at peace. I will try to continue without you. Even though the thought of being here every day without you fills me with despair. You changed the lives of everyone you knew and will change many more. I'm so proud of the girl you were, in spite of everything, and that gorgeous smile is imprinted in my brain.

I made a scrapbook of all our pictures and wrote down every single thing I remember from the day we met to the day you left because I don't want to forget a single second. Not even the pain when the plate you threw hit me in the face, lolz. I know you will always be by my side until we are reunited. I can barely breathe and I can't take the pain, you always were my everything. One day, we will be together again. Forever.

Bye bye baby. You always were the hardest act to follow my love.

If Kitten could have spoken, I'm sure her last words would have been: 'I like big tits, and I cannot lie.' Haha.

My daughter, Kitten, was sensitive, loyal, and intelligent. She could be really stubborn. But she was playful and so kind, compassionate, and caring. I've never known anyone with such pure intentions. She will be greatly missed.

—Dr Anthony Markus, Kitten's dad

I just want to give a massive shout-out of gratefulness to Kit's big bro, Dan.

You came in late, but it was you who had the biggest impact on her. She let you in so easily, you are the only person she didn't try to push away. Amy and I saved her from the darkness. The son of Zeus saved her life… But by loving her, you healed the damage done by sewer rat and all the other males that hurt her. You healed her broken heart.

The impact you had was truly monumental. You argue that it was mainly me, but in all honesty, out of everything, the best thing I ever did for Kitten was finding you and bringing you into our lives. You made the last part of her life so happy and filled with joy, and even when you left you still kept us close and found people to help her. I suspect she loved you. I'm really stoked she got to experience that before she died. When I saw you together at drums, your connection, I understood: you belong. She was always mine alone, until I found you. Then she was *our* sweet little Angel. You made her so happy! To be able to make someone who has been hurt that badly, feel so at ease is testament to your lovely heart. You are one hell of a man.

Luv, Tiger.
X

Email: divineangelcounselling1@outlook.com

www.ingramcontent.com/pod-product-compliance
Lightning Source LLC
Chambersburg PA
CBHW070349120526
44590CB00014B/1069